The Steinway Hunter

The Steinway Hunter

Experience the Travels of the Man Who Brought Thousands of Steinway Pianos Back to the Market and the People and Places He Encountered Along the Way

Robert Friedman

with
Ronnie Rosenberg-Friedman

Epigraph
BOOKS
RHINEBECK, NEW YORK

Copyright © 2019 by Robert G. Friedman and Ronnie Rosenberg-Friedman
Copyright Registration Number TXu002137011 / Date: 2019-02-21

All rights reserved. Published 2019.

No portion of this book may be reproduced in any fashion, print, facsimile, or electronic, or by any method yet to be developed, without the express written permission of the publisher.

Epigraph Books
22 E Market Street, Suite 304
Rhinebeck, NY 12572

Most of the names used in these stories are real people, written about them with their permission. Due to the passage of time, I have forgotten some of the names of the people in the stories, so I've creatively re-named them.

For more information write to SteinwayHunter@gmail.com

Paperback: 978-1-7337670-0-2
eBook: 978-1-7337670-1-9
Hardcover (with dust jacket): 978-1-7337670-2-6
Library of Congress Control Number: 2019917899

Cover photo and design, and book design by Barbara Aronica-Buck
Illustrations by Ronnie Rosenberg-Friedman

Manufactured in the United States of America

Dedicated to
The Steinway Family

Contents

Acknowledgments	ix
About the Cover	xi
Foreword	xiii
Preface	xv
1. The First Hunt: "Rhapsody for Mr. Blue"	1
2. The Key to My Future	7
3. Dawn of the Steinway Hunter	15
4. From First Bass	24
5. Thanks from 35,000 Feet	31
6. Burned Out in Buffalo	35
7. From Monk to Master	43
8. Amsterdam Fireman	47
9. The Lady's Friend Must Stay	54
10. The Steinway on the Wall	60
11. Almost the Last Tennessee Waltz	63
12. Off the Notches	68
13. When the Angels Sang to the Clydesdales	74
14. 62554	79

15. O My Shoulder	92
16. Tall, Dark, and Handy	98
17. The Library B	105
18. Monkey Bid	108
19. Nepper Nepperland	116
20. Rach's Wrap	121
21. Lost in Groundhog Town	124
22. Amber Waves Good-bye to Misty	128
23. Buy a Steinway, Save a House	134
24. The Wallpapered Steinway Secret	138
25. From Behind the Curtain	140
About the Author	143

Acknowledgments

I'm grateful to all the piano designers, engineers, manufacturers, salespeople, and piano movers who have worked so hard, for so long, to build this industry. Also, to all of the tuner/technicians and rebuilders, who make sure that the pianos of the world are kept in proper playing order.

I could not have done it without my mother, who gave me vital information from her many years in newspaper advertising. She taught me how to utilize those skills, along with telephone communications, to explore the vast frontier of piano hunting. Also, my father; without his love of playing the piano, I would never have known how much joy it could bring to a truly romantic pianist.

My children, Michael, Jason, Kimberly, Chelsea, and Joel, gave me the desire, and the need, to succeed in my journey of bringing these musical treasures back to the marketplace. Their encouragement as it unfolded reinforced my desire to write this book.

I'm thankful to my wife, Ronnie, for sharing her creative ideas. Her help in story development and editing kept the stories interesting and straightforward. With her love and support inspiring me, I gained the courage to put this book forth.

My most sincere thanks to Leslie Wells for her help with editing. Throughout the writing process, with her suggestions, she helped to make these stories bloom.

With the final copyediting by Kate Petrella, the finishing touches were put on the book. Thank you, Kate!

Jon Regen consistently pushed me onto the correct path with his friendship and enthusiasm. He has been a key motivator for me to complete this book. I cannot thank him enough.

Thanks to my friend Rick Dawson, my pianos reached their destinations safely.

I am forever grateful to Michael and Nicole Rutsky for their friendship and loyalty.

Shortly after the invention of the internet came the birth of www.pianomart.com, by owner Joseph Ross. Joe single-handedly created the platform for the world's leading online trading floor for pianos. With the use of pianomart.com, I've managed to connect with thousands of Steinway owners. Along with his help and friendship, my hunt for Steinways has evolved.

Vince Leone, Henry Kerren, Peter Hume, and Ed Glatzel were instrumental in helping me realize my potential by offering their lifelong, well-developed technical, personal, and business skills in the piano industry.

Throughout the centuries following Bartolomeo Cristofori's invention of the instrument, the industry has brought new materials and many innovative ways to restore, market, and keep pianos singing to their fullest. I'm honored to have worked with people who are, in my opinion, the best of the best, the ones I consider the Keepers of the Keys: Jeffrey Baker, Luis Cajas, Joseph Hanerfeld, James Fullmer, Al Ammon, Shawn Hoar, Dale Erwin, Larry Buck, and William "Maestro Bruno" Santo.

And finally, to Murray Rosenberg, for bringing me piano good luck!

About the Cover

Barbara called me to sell her mother's Steinway grand. She told me that her mother had recently passed away and she was getting her house ready to sell. She also told me that she wanted to keep the piano in the house until it sold, so as not to have a big empty space in the spot where it sat. Grand pianos are good for staging a house, and Barbara knew it. We agreed that if it was a piano I wanted to buy, I wouldn't have it removed until the house was sold.

As I do with most purchases these days, I didn't go to her mother's home to see the piano but asked her to email a series of photos for me to review. I told her I had specific written criteria, which was backed up by sample photos of a Steinway grand piano for her to follow. She agreed and assured me the photos would be no problem for her, since she was a book designer and had a vast knowledge of photography.

Once she told me she was a book designer, I told her about the book I had been working on for over forty years about my adventures on the road buying Steinways.

A few days later, I received her email. Her late mother's piano was a 1923 Steinway model M 5'7" grand, traditional style in Indonesian mahogany.

What I did not expect were much better views of the piano in her photos than I normally received. There was one photo in particular that I was excited to see, which made all the other photos worthwhile.

That photo is the cover of this book.

Foreword

My first contact with the Steinway Hunter occurred about twenty-five years ago. I saw an ad in the classified section of my local newspaper that read "Steinway Grand Piano Wanted! Any Age, Any Condition." I called the number in the ad and spoke to Bob Friedman, who would later become known as "the Steinway Hunter." Through the years, he would also become a good friend.

We spoke on the phone several times before our first face-to-face meeting, which came several months later. At that first meeting, Bob and I hit it off immediately. Bob is an easygoing guy who laughs often, is unpretentious and has the ability to put one at ease. I think we both recognized the fact that we were in the presence of a kindred spirit. We were about the same age, we were both piano technicians, we liked the same kind of music, and we were both amateur performing musicians. Our strongest connection, however, was the fact that we are both passionate about pianos!

But what drives this passion? Perhaps it is the fact that, to people who love pianos, they are more than simply a musical instrument constructed of wood, metal, felt, wire, and steel. Metaphorically, they are living beings, each with its own character and personality and each one capable of expressing the complete palette of human emotion including happiness, joy, sadness, and pain. The average life span of a piano is about seventy-five to one hundred years. If a piano could talk, what would it say? What has it witnessed in its lifetime? Whose fingers have played it? How many times has someone played "Happy Birthday" on it? How many children have learned to love music through its ivory keys? Has it been neglected in a cold, dark, damp basement for the last fifty years, or has it graced the stage of one of the world's most prestigious concert halls? In this book, Bob gives a voice to some of those pianos and we learn the answer to some of those questions.

Musically Yours,
Joe Ross
Founder, PianoMart.com
Piano Technicians Guild
Registered Piano Technician

Preface

Through the years, some people in my industry who know me well and some people whose pianos have found new homes with my help have suggested that I write a book about my travels hunting for Steinways. The first time I located and sold a piano was in 1971. From that first piano buy the stories began. The tale that unfolded from each locate made the journey and the people who were involved in the process part of the history of that piano. Although the methods have evolved, the events of the past forty-plus years are the reason I'm still strongly involved in the business that I started.

Through nationwide advertising, consistent networking, and endless hours of driving in some of the most treacherous weather, I have done more to expand the vintage Steinway piano market than anyone else. I have made thousands of Steinway pianos available to be restored by the finest piano restoration experts in the world and to ultimately find a new home.

I hope you enjoy the read as much as I enjoyed the write.

All the best . . .
Bob Friedman

Chapter 1
THE FIRST HUNT: "RHAPSODY FOR MR. BLUE"

The year was 1971. I was seventeen years old, one month away from graduating from high school. It was late spring. I remember that because the weather was just getting warm after being consistently cool outside. I was living with my parents in an apartment complex in Poughkeepsie, a small upstate New York town on the Hudson River. This is where I was born, and it was the town I knew as my home. I was blessed with two loving parents, who raised not only me but my sister, who was thirteen years my senior, and a cousin who was five years older than I was.

Francis, who was my second cousin from my father's side of the family, came to live with my parents at the age of four, after his mother passed away, one year before I was born. He never knew his father. We all called him Butch, and as far as I knew, he was my brother.

My sister was nicknamed Cookie, because from the time she was a toddler she loved cookies, but her real name was Rochelle. She married at the age of eighteen and soon started a family, making me an uncle at six years old. She had three children, Tony, Cathy, and Jimmy. Since I was close in age to her children, it was like having younger siblings.

A family in the same garden apartment complex, right behind where we were living, was selling their dad's piano. He had just passed away. We lived on the second floor, they lived on the first floor, and therefore we had a balcony and they had a patio facing the same common area. From our balcony, I could see a sign posted outside of their door that read, "House sale, everything must go." I was unfamiliar with people selling their personal property due to a death in the family. I felt sad for their loss, especially during such a beautiful time of year.

I went down to the back door of their apartment, where the sign was posted. The door was open, so I peeked inside and was greeted by the daughter of the man who had just passed. She asked me if I would like to come in and look around. I replied "Yes, if it would be okay with you," and she let me in.

There were many fine pieces of furniture as well as pictures and glassware that looked like they had been collected by someone with a great love of decorating. I glanced to my right, and there stood a dream come true for my father: an upright piano. I hoped it was for sale. It was very tall, oak in color with beautiful ivory keys, and the name "Sohmer & Co., New York" was over the keys. It looked ready to be played, and I felt that I had to make sure that my father would be the next to make it sing.

I asked the girl if the piano was for sale, and she replied, "Yes." I was very excited. At the time, I knew very little about pianos, except that my father played very well, and deserved to have a piano in our home for his enjoyment. I asked the girl how much she was selling the piano for, and she replied that it was two hundred dollars. I thought

The First Hunt: "Rhapsody for Mr. Blue" 3

that it was a very good price for such a handsome instrument. I asked her if she would give me a moment to run home and tell my parents, so my father could come over and try it. She said that she would not sell it to anyone until I came back.

I ran home, thrilled to tell my mother what I had discovered. She was very excited and hoped my father would be too. When my father got home from work, we told him about the piano, but he didn't seem eager to see it.

The problem was that at age thirteen, my father had been planning a career in music as a classical pianist. This was told to me by my grandmother, my father's mother, after his passing; I never knew this while he was alive. A child virtuoso, he was accepted by a very well-known agent who was to introduce him to the big time. But because my father, although highly skilled, was insecure at that young age and refused to perform without his music in front of him, he was released by his agent. He felt that he needed the music in front of him as a safety net when he played. However, memorizing the music was a requirement if you were to be a concert pianist. He never attempted to climb the ladder of success as a concert pianist again. During his twenties, he began working in the floor-covering industry, and remained in that trade until his death.

By the time I found the two-hundred-dollar piano, he was fifty-five years old. In many ways he was bitter about the events of his youth when it came to playing or even owning a piano. I could see that he didn't feel good about treating himself to one. He never talked to me about the pain that he experienced as a young man, so I asked my mother why he was so negative about having a piano in our home. All she could tell me was that when I was two years old, in 1956, my father gave his childhood piano to his sister, who lived nearby. The only time I ever heard him play was at her house during family get-togethers. He never told my mother about the regrets of his youth and the reason he gave up his piano. These few times I got to see and hear him play, his eyes would light up and he seemed to be soaring in a rainbow of music.

Now, I was determined that he have the opportunity to do what he seemed to love so much. My mother demanded that he go and see what looked like a wonderful piano. Finally, he agreed to look at it.

We walked down our stairs, around the back of our apartment and over to the home where the piano was. Again, we were greeted by the girl.

I said, "I'd like to introduce you to my father, Howard Friedman."

She responded, "It's very nice to meet you, sir."

She led us to the piano. My father sat down, put his hands to the keys and played that piano, seeming happy in a way that I rarely saw him.

At that moment, I suspected he was going to bring the piano home. He asked the girl if he could take a little time to decide, and he would let her know the next day. She said that would be fine. We went home, and he discussed it with my mother, but he was having a hard time with the thought of treating himself to the piano. I became angry with him because my mother and I felt, as he did not, that he deserved to have a piano. After all, he'd worked so hard to learn how to play at that level.

Later that evening, I went over to a friend's house in the same complex. There, two of my best friends, Dave Gesh and David Meister, and I sat around, as we often did, jamming on acoustic guitars. Our favorites were by Crosby, Stills, Nash and Young. We imagined that we were at Woodstock together, but sadly, none of us had attended that famous concert.

The next day, my father finally agreed to purchase the piano. Several days later, it was moved up into our apartment. Once he had it tuned, he played it almost every evening when he came home from work.

There was one little defect in this piano, but he never complained about it. One key in the high treble section, located in the last octave, did not work properly. Late one afternoon while he was at work, I took the front panel off the piano, which covered most of the action, or the working parts inside. Since I was mechanically inclined, this didn't scare me. My major in high school was industrial arts. I was in the top of all my classes, whether it be woodworking, metal fabrication, pattern-making, mechanical drafting, or architectural blueprint design.

Within the action of the piano, there was a spring that belonged underneath a jack-type lever that had popped out of place. This spring was needed to help the key return, so that it was ready for the next time it was played. All of the other eighty-seven springs were in place. I took a pair of needle-nose pliers and very carefully pushed down on the spring, placing it back in the hole under the jack. Immediately, the key returned, and was ready to be played. My mother came into the living room, and to her surprise saw I had taken apart the piano.

She gasped and asked, "What are you doing?"

"I just fixed the key that wasn't working properly," I explained.

She smiled at me and replied, "Well, that's a very good thing, but can you please put it back together before your father gets home?"

About an hour later, my father got home from work. First, he sat in his easy chair to read the local paper. Shortly after that, we sat down to dinner. After dinner, we joked around a little, then he went to play the piano. My father was a funny man and we enjoyed quipping with each other. One thing I realized was that now that he again had a piano in his life, he seemed much more relaxed and satisfied with himself.

I watched him very carefully, waiting for a change in his expression, once his fingers played the key that I'd fixed. As he played in that section and hit that key, he did a slight double-take before he continued to play. I'm sure that he realized the key was working, but never said anything about it. That would have been the moment to tell him that I had fixed the key, but instead, I let it pass. When he was finished playing that night, it was late, and I was satisfied with the fact that I had fixed it, but I didn't feel the need to tell him. I wanted it to remain a mystery.

My fascination with piano technology began with the repair I made to his piano. At the same time, my interest in piano sales was launched. I knew how happy it made him to finally have a piano to play. It seemed as if he never really forgot his dream of being the best of the best. Throughout my career buying and selling Steinways, I look back on this event often and realize that my work is not just a paycheck for me, but a way to bring happiness to people.

My father passed away suddenly on May 31, 1974, at just fifty-eight years old; only three years after he had allowed himself to play the piano again.

Chapter 2

THE KEY TO MY FUTURE

It was three years after my father's passing, and I was still interested in the idea of getting involved with pianos. I was twenty-three years old, living with my first wife and my newborn son, Michael, working for my friend Dave painting houses. Searching through the help wanted section of our local newspaper, *The Poughkeepsie Journal*, I saw an ad that read, "Piano and organ salesmen wanted. No previous keyboard sales experience necessary but must play the piano. Contact Jim Shanahan at The Keyboard Center, Fishkill, New York" and it gave the phone number. I thought to myself, "I can do this."

From the time my father brought that first piano into our home, I would sit at it and teach myself to play. I believed that I possessed everything it took to become a great piano salesman. After all, I had convinced a man who quit playing the piano for most of his life to buy one, fixed the key that didn't work, and I learned to play.

I called Jim at The Keyboard Center, which was in the Dutchess Mall, one of the first indoor malls in the northeast, and made an appointment. We met later that day and we instantly hit it off.

He hired me and trained me in every facet of piano and organ sales.

Jim taught me about the moving parts of the piano, how they worked, and the materials that were used to make them. There were a variety of upright and grand pianos that we sold in the store; Mason & Hamlin, Kohler & Campbell, Kawai, and Kincaid, but no Steinways.

We also sold Thomas organs. During a long training period I learned how to play and demonstrate the entire line, which consisted of ten models. Thomas Organs were famous, having been used on *The Lawrence Welk Show*, a well-known weekly television variety show. It was also the only organ that had the patented "Color Glow" feature. This feature was engineered to make the entire keyboard light up, and the keys were marked with the note of the key, to help beginners memorize the keyboard. It was a magnificent invention that helped thousands of people learn to play the organ.

In no time, I was selling pianos and organs like a pro. I proved to Jim that I was a great asset, so much so that he offered me the position of assistant manager. Along with this position came more responsibilities. I would have to make sure the store always looked good, vacuum as often as possible, dust the instruments, and keep the massive wall of sheet music in order. Basically, everything I was used to helping with before, I was now responsible for. I was also expected to train part-time salespeople whenever Jim hired them. Jim and I worked split shifts, with one of us always there to cover the floor. The hours were long and tiring. The store was open 9 a.m. to 9 p.m., Monday through Saturday, and 10 a.m. to 6 p.m. on Sundays.

This was the only store in our company's nine-store chain in New York state. The other eight stores were scattered throughout the state of Connecticut. This made it difficult to have the company's sole piano tuner visit often enough to keep our instruments in tune.

Jim called a few tuners he found in the local yellow pages. A few of our pianos were tuned by them, but we weren't satisfied with the work. One day Jim barked at me, "Why don't you learn to tune pianos, so I don't have to keep looking for someone to do it?" I replied, "I'd love to, but who's going to teach me?"

Shortly thereafter, Jim called Vince Leone, the best tuner-tech in our area. Ever since I'd lost my father a few years before, I was hopeful that I would meet a man that I could look up to, and possibly learn from. Vince was the one who helped me get started with my career in piano technology, and he treated me like a son while he was teaching me.

He came to the store often. While he was there tuning, we would talk and joke, and we became friends. He was very close to my father's age, so it was easy for me to bond with him as a father figure. He was semi-retired from the piano business, and during our conversations, he told me his history in the piano industry.

Early in his career, he worked as a tuner for Steinway in New York, where he learned to regulate piano actions, along with tuning. He moved to the Poughkeepsie area in the 1950s, bought a piece of property on a major highway, and built a piano store, where he was very successful for twenty-five years. A few years before we met, he closed the store and sold the property, although he still tuned pianos locally.

Vince would often say, "I'd like to fully retire, but I keep getting called back to work." I'd reply, "So teach me!" He told me that he preferred in-home tunings, rather than store tunings. The store expected to get a break on pricing, because he would tune four or five at a time, and that made it hardly worth his while.

While closing his toolbox one day, he looked at me and asked me if I was ready to learn. I replied, "Yes!" He said, "Meet me at nine tomorrow morning and we'll get started."

The next day at the store, he walked me over to an old brown console piano. He took off the front panel and reached for a tool from his toolbox.

He handed me the tool and said, "Give me fifteen dollars."

I asked, "What for?"

He said, "You want to learn, don't you?"

I replied, "Yes."

Again, he said, "Give me fifteen dollars!"

I took out a twenty-dollar bill, handed it to him, and he gave me back a five-dollar bill. Then he said, "Watch what I do with this tool."

Vince was holding an identical tool in his hand, but it was much newer, and in better condition. He placed it at the back of the key, stuck it through a small round hole at the top of a dowel that was connected to the key, and turned it clockwise.

He told me to watch as the key became level with the one to the right of it. He explained to me that everywhere in the action of a piano, where wood touches wood, there's a piece of felt to prevent the wood from knocking together. After the piano gets played for a long time, the felts become packed down, and the action goes out of regulation. This causes lost motion in the keys. With this tool, you adjust the action to lessen the lost motion. My interest had been piqued.

He packed up his toolbox and said, "I'll meet you here the same time tomorrow."

The next day we had a similar go-round. He opened his toolbox, took out a different tool, handed it to me and said, as he had the day before, "Give me fifteen dollars."

I smiled and took out a twenty, and he gave me the change.

He held the same tool, but newer than the one he had just

handed to me. He pointed to a different spot in the action of the same piano and said, "Watch what I do with this tool." After he was done, he said, "Do the same thing I did to the key to the right of it."

I followed his instructions exactly. He patted me on the shoulder, letting me know he was satisfied with me and said, "Meet me here tomorrow, same time."

On the third day, a Friday, we repeated the same process, Vince selling me an old tool and showing me a new skill in piano repair.

At the end of this session, he said, "On Monday morning I want to start you out with the most important thing you'll need to learn, but it will take years to perfect."

I shook his hand to thank him, and assured him, "I'll be here, ready to learn."

On Monday, instead of his toolbox, he carried a small leather bag. He opened it and took out an old piano tuning hammer and four rubber wedges. He handed them all to me, including the bag he carried in, and said, "This time I want twenty-five dollars."

I took the tuning hammer and the wedges and handed him the money.

He looked at me and said, "You don't need me any more."

"What?"

He repeated, "You don't need me any more."

I told him, "I can't tune a piano."

He smiled. "But you will learn."

He continued, "You've watched me for almost a year now. You have good ears, and you can play the piano. I've given you plenty of tips about making the adjustments that a piano needs to play correctly, and you can do it. Now, learn to tune them. I'm done here. It's up to you now."

I was stunned at how Vince had thrown me out onto the playing field.

He came in from time to time to check up on me, and to see how I was coming along. When he did, I would take him to the back of the store, where we kept the old upright pianos that were taken in on trade. These were the pianos that I used to practice on, learning how to tune. Eventually I had the confidence to go onto the selling floor, where I would tune the new ones.

After I'd spent four years as a salesman at The Keyboard Center, the owners of the chain encountered financial difficulties. Jim and I got the bad news one day that the store would be closing soon. I needed to plan, if I was going to stay in the piano business.

A few days after we got that news, two tractor-trailers pulled up to the back of the store. They were there to load up all the instruments that we had on the sales floor. The owners had stopped paying the inventory financing, so their creditors were taking over the stock. The only pianos they didn't take were a few old uprights that needed restoration, at the back of the store. I later moved them to a storage unit for safekeeping.

After they loaded up all the pianos and organs, Jim and I just looked at each other. The keyboard business we'd worked so hard to establish together was taken away.

During that time, my son and I were living with my mother, as my marriage had dissolved six months before. I was still interested in pursuing my work with pianos. I needed to find shop space where I could work on the instruments I had in storage, in addition to acquiring new piano projects to work on. I was unable to locate a suitable space and was becoming frustrated, so my mother offered me the use of her living room while I continued to search. Having only two pianos at the time, I took her up on it.

Along with a few friends, one who had a pickup truck, I moved the pianos into my mother's small one-bedroom apartment. Michael and I slept on a big fold-out couch.

In the evenings, I played drums in a rock-and-roll band, and sometimes got home as the sun was coming up. My mother worked at a local newspaper and began her workday at 9 a.m. She needed to be out the door by 8 a.m. Before she left for work on the days that I had played the night before, she would feed breakfast to Michael, then age 14 months old, while I slept.

One morning I woke up with Michael fast asleep beside me. All seemed well, until I walked around the apartment to discover that he had turned anything and everything he possibly could upside down. The refrigerator was wide open, with food on the floor in front of it. Some of the plants in the living room were toppled over, with dirt on the floor. The cat's litter box in the bathroom was dumped over, and my guitar had been knocked off its stand. The tools that Vince had sold me were lying on the floor, with the tuning hammer hanging off the edge of a piano bench, as though Michael had been trying to tune the instrument. It must have been very noisy, but I had slept through it all, and Michael, having spent his energy, had crept back into bed.

After a few weeks, I fixed and sold both pianos. I was still hunting for the perfect shop space, but had no luck finding exactly what I wanted, so my mother insisted that I continue using her apartment until I did.

This time I moved in four upright pianos. Once I fixed and sold two of them, I moved in an old 5'3" grand piano. It was a 1926 Stultz & Bauer. This was the first piano I ever replaced plastic key-tops on. It was a painful experience. I removed the old chipped and cracked ivory key-tops with a boxcutter blade by candlelight during an electrical blackout, bloodying my hands.

It had become ridiculously crowded in my poor mother's small apartment. Something needed to change. Soon after that group of pianos sold, I finally found and rented a small space in the back of a glass shop in Red Oaks Mill, New York. It was close to where The Keyboard Center had been, so it felt right. I began buying, fixing, and reselling old upright pianos that I bought locally.

I continued to hone my skills. I restored the cases, retapped the tuning pins, replaced old rusty strings, repaired the broken keys, glued cracks in soundboards, replaced broken, worn-out felt hammers, and tuned them the best I knew how.

Once the shop was set up and running, I called Vince to ask him if he would come over and tune a few pianos for me. He was more than happy to help. I paid him much better than they did at The Keyboard Center. He stuck by me until I started making the kind of money I needed to keep things rolling smoothly. From time to time, he would also ask for my help when he needed to move a piano that he bought for resale. Even in retirement, he would buy and sell a few pianos a month out of his home and go out and tune a few more.

Without the help of Vince and Jim, along with my experience from working at The Keyboard Center, I might not have entered into the piano business.

Chapter 3

DAWN OF THE STEINWAY HUNTER

One of the smartest men I have ever met in the piano business once told me to look at the brands of pianos that I was dealing; that would dictate how much money I could earn. In the years following our first meeting, this old-time piano man became my friend and mentor. His valuable knowledge in the world of piano dealing, along with his words of wisdom about the people I would encounter, helped me to develop my passion for hunting Steinways.

The first time I met Henry was on the phone. I advertised a low-end brand of spinet piano for sale, along with the price I was asking. At the time, I was living in Poughkeepsie, New York, which is located on the east side of the Hudson River. He advertised the same brand, with no price listed, where he lived in Kingston, New York, on the west side of the river. This happened a few times within a month or two. I finally called him and introduced myself. We got along well over the phone, joking about our piano buying and selling tales, and sharing simple technical information about the different brands. I could tell that he was quite a bit older than I was with much more experience in the piano industry than I had, but I had no problem keeping up with him. At that time, I had ten years of experience buying, selling, and reconditioning most brands of pianos. Through our many conversations, I felt as though he heard a younger version of himself in me. The one thing I never brought up in our first conversation was the real reason I called him, which was to find out why he wasn't putting prices in the paper when he advertised his pianos.

I asked him where he bought most of his pianos, and he replied, "Probably the same places you do." It wasn't the answer that I expected or wanted. One thing he would not do is give up his business information over the phone. He knew that that's what I was after, and he was not giving up his secrets.

I told him that I had more console and spinet pianos, of all brands, than I had time to fix or sell. I wondered if he would be interested in buying a bunch of them from me, cheap. He said, "You mean wholesale?" I said, "If that's the term, yes." He asked if I would deliver them as well, and I said yes.

I described the condition of the pianos to him in detail, along with the brands and serial numbers. After some negotiating, we agreed on a price, including delivery. It sounded as though we had developed a level of trust between us. We set a time for the next day when I would deliver the pianos to his shop.

The next afternoon I drove to Henry's small garage shop, which was located next to his house. As he walked out to meet me, he looked over at me and my two young sons—Jason, age six, and Michael, ten—who rode along with me and were sitting in the back of my old American Motors Matador station wagon. Behind that I was dragging a beat-up U-Haul double-axle trailer loaded with pianos. He nodded me a greeting, then shook his head. I think he thought I needed guidance.

Henry looked as though he was in his late sixties. He had a striking resemblance to the actor Jimmy Cagney. It was apparent that he immediately took a liking to me, as I did him.

With a strong handshake, we introduced ourselves. I walked to the back of my trailer and opened it, so that he could look at the four pianos that I had described to him the day before. After a quick inspection, he said, "Let's move them in."

He reached for his old, beat-up blue piano dolly. It looked as though it must have been with him for many years. I noticed that the wheels were fairly new, even though the paint on the top, along with the rubber rails, was worn almost through to the wood. I asked him how long that old dolly had been with him. He looked me in the eye and said, "Longer than you've been alive."

Now, having spent over forty years in the same line of work that he was in, I could understand the relationship he had with that old dolly. Even though I don't move pianos any more, I still have one of my favorite old dollies; one that's been with me since the beginning. If you are as serious about your work as Henry was, and as I am, your dolly becomes one of your most valuable tools.

My sons got out of the car and came to the back of the trailer to help me untie the many ropes and knots. I over-tied the pianos to keep them from moving while in transit. Once the ropes and the old bed blankets were removed, Henry transferred the pianos to his blue dolly, one at a time, and we moved them into his shop.

During this first meeting he introduced me to his wife, Carol, who was also his business partner. Later in our relationship, I discovered that she was also a very good piano tuner-technician. They made a perfect team.

This first face-to-face meeting was during the spring of 1987. Even though we shared a lot of interesting marketing and technical ideas about the piano business, I felt that there was still some distance that he kept between us. I was thirty-three at the time, so he was old enough to be my father. He wanted to make sure I could be trusted with the knowledge he would offer me, and not use it to compete with him in our local market.

I knew the local used piano market was a good one, and if you priced your reconditioned pianos low enough, they would sell quickly. He also knew this, and since we weren't partners, we both needed to keep our pricing a secret from the other until the ads in the papers came out. We both advertised in the same papers, so sometimes it made for a price battle between us. I would travel much farther and wider, and bought more used pianos than he did. He bought most of his locally.

Within a few months of our first meeting, we established an arrangement. He would buy used console and spinet pianos from me, and I would deliver them to him at wholesale prices. I also agreed not to advertise in his backyard. This way, I could sell my inventory much quicker, in bulk, but at lower prices, without having to do any work on them, other than the buying and moving.

My wholesale piano career was born. Henry had offered me a way to move at a speed that I enjoyed, and the little bit of money that I had to work with would stay in motion.

After a few months of doing business this way, he invited me to work beside him and Carol, in their home shop, helping them to recondition some of the pianos that I had sold him. They knew that I had many years of professional piano selling experience, working as a piano and organ salesman in a local mall, so they also asked me to meet with some of their clients and sell for them.

Henry had it all figured out. He now had a full-time buyer, selling wholesale pianos to him, with delivery included; a part-time piano tech; and a piano salesman, all in one. I, on the other hand, also had it good. I continued to buy and sell pianos from my home, as well as working with him.

One day while we were working and joking around in his shop, I asked him why, when we first met, he would advertise similar pianos to mine for sale in the same papers, without prices. He replied, "Does Macy's tell Gimbels?"

As we became better friends, the three of us would pick a day, go out to dinner and share the piano news of our week. I was mostly busy with my family and running around buying pianos for Henry and for myself. I had very little time to hang out with him, except when we were rushing to prepare a piano for sale, or I was moving some in for them. Still, we found time in between for some good laughs. Our best times were when he would tell me his old piano war stories. He had some of the best I'd ever heard.

One was about the time when, in his early thirties, he was working as a piano tuner for a small-town dealer in North Carolina. He answered a call from an old woman who wanted to sell her Steinway grand. He said that that was a rare call, because there were not many Steinway grand pianos in that neck of the woods.

The owner of the store took the phone from Henry and asked the woman her name and address, so he could send his tuner to look at it, to see if they'd be interested in buying it. After he had the address written on a piece of paper, he handed it to Henry. The owner kept the woman on the phone, talking about the piano, as Henry drove over to her house. While she was still on the phone with the owner of the store, Henry knocked on the door. She hung up the phone and answered the door. Henry introduced himself as the tuner for the piano store. She invited Henry in to see the piano. Of course, he made the purchase, and she never had a chance to call another dealer.

When we would joke and make comments about other people in the piano business, whether it be salespeople, tuners, or manufacturers, he would say, "If we're talking about them, I'm sure they're talking about us. We don't need to care what they're saying; as long as we are doing it right, we don't need to waste our time wondering. But one thing is for sure, when someone says something about someone, there's something going on."

Many years after our conversation about the people in our industry talking about each other behind their backs, I coined the phrase "Junior High Piano Party."

During the next few years I sold Henry many pianos, including a few old Steinway uprights from the 1890s. These pianos were very ornate, with round, reeded column-type legs. They also had carved-out decorative panels in the front, covering the hammer action. Each time I offered him a Steinway he got very excited, much more so than when he bought any other brand from me. Even though they needed more work to bring them back to good playing order, and to make them look good, because they were so old and beat up, he still wanted them. He even paid me twice what he had been paying me for the pianos that weren't Steinways. That was when I realized what was going on.

I had always heard that Steinway was the brand that serious pianists preferred and would pay more for. I rarely purchased them because the cost was more than I could afford to spend just in the hope that a buyer who would have the money would come along. My business model at that time was buy them cheap, fix them quick, and sell them fast. That was the market that I understood.

Henry asked me to supply him with more Steinway uprights. He said that he had enough off-brands to sell. As I saw it, the world was overstocked with every other brand but Steinway, and Henry knew that I was on to that.

After two years of selling pianos to him, he sat me down and said, "You know what to do now. Stop dealing with the other brands and just stick to Steinway; this is where the money is. It's the only way you'll make enough money to support yourself and your family in the piano business."

On that day, with his blessing, I drove out of his driveway and made my decision to hunt Steinways.

The first thing I had to do was get a toll-free telephone number. The next thing was to place ads in the local papers to buy Steinway pianos. Since I was just starting out with this new venture, my cash flow was very limited. I figured Steinway grand pianos needing restoration was the way to go. Most of the restored Steinways were being sold by piano shops in New York City. If I were to wholesale them quickly to keep the money in motion, I had to meet with these shop owners to find out what they were willing to pay for Steinways in need of restoration.

Once most of the dealers I met with said they were interested, I began researching where I could get a list of all the daily and weekly newspapers throughout New York State. Since my mother was very successful in this field and had been involved in almost every phase of commercial and classified advertising, I went to her for advice.

Her biggest claim to fame was achieved in 1982, while she was employed by *The Poughkeepsie Journal*, our local daily newspaper. This paper was owned by the Gannett Company, which has one of the largest advertising networks in the world. In that year, Gannett founded *USA Today*. My mother and three of her co-workers, also women, were chosen to design the very first layout for the classified network, some of which is still used today. Her knowledge in this field made her a tremendous asset to me.

She first pointed me in the direction of the local library. There, she said, I would find the *Gale Book of Publications*. At that time, this was the encyclopedia of advertising. All the publications I needed to run my ads were in there.

Off to the library I went. I spent almost a week there the first time, listing all the papers in New York, Connecticut, Massachusetts, and New Jersey. One state at a time, I ran my ads, which read, "Steinway Grand Piano Wanted! Any Age, Any Condition, Will Pay Cash and Pick Up," along with my toll-free number. After two weeks of these ads running in all the weekly and daily papers in New York State, the phone started to ring with Steinway owners wanting to sell. With Henry's life-changing suggestion, and my mother's influence in advertising, my hunt for Steinways started and never stopped.

After a few years of being on the road, traveling most of the U.S., buying and supplying as many Steinways as I could find to every rebuilder that needed them, I decided to take a short break. I visited with Henry and Carol a few times between my trips to let them know that his suggestion about sticking to Steinways was a financially life-changing idea.

On one occasion when I visited, he told me that he was very pleased with how I managed the work. With a big grin, he looked me in the eye and said, "If I was a younger man, I would get in that truck with you, and become your partner." After all, he knew it was his good advice that I was following, and he had every right to ride shotgun. We both knew he was not going to leave Carol and live the life I was, sleeping along interstate highways and in cheap hotels, eating in between Steinway buys and sleeping when I had the time. He was quite comfortable where he was, living a life of ease, dealing pianos locally.

I, on the other hand, had many years of Steinway hunting in front of me, with many mouths to feed. Eventually, my family grew to a whopping five children on the scene. My second wife was a stay-at-home mom who made sure the children were well taken care of while I was on the road. Most of the hunts were from five to seven days, with some trips lasting as long as eleven days. That went on for nearly three decades. The good news, for me and my family, was that in between each trip I was home for more than two weeks at a time. This gave us lots of quality time together, whether we were taking the girls to dance lessons, events at school, birthday parties, concerts in the local parks, or just staying at home in the pool. The boys were also very busy, going to baseball, soccer, and tennis practices and games, not to mention all the birthday parties that their friends would invite them to. I made sure that I did not miss any of the most important moments in all their lives as they were growing up.

Looking back now, I realize how fortunate I was to have met that old man who was once my local competition, and who shared with me his powerful wisdom. In my heart and soul, he was the greatest of all the piano men I've known.

Chapter 4

FROM FIRST BASS

For every great accomplishment we experience, will there also be a terrible loss we must endure? My very first long-distance Steinway road trip started with that heart-wrenching question.

Growing up in a small upstate New York town was lots of fun in the late 1960s and early 1970s. Most of my friends were self-taught wannabe rock-and-roll stars with dreams of becoming part of the big music scene, but with no plan at all. Yet we practiced, we wrote good songs, and we performed locally for a few decades in dirty old bars for hardly any money. And, we always looked the part, thanks to Kenny, "The Doctor of Hair."

I was drawn to playing the drums. In my early teens, I was always beating out rhythms that had a catchy groove on just about everything from my knees to a kitchen table, until I finally had real drums to play on. Fortunately for me, I was surrounded by many good musicians. I was able to hook up with some of them and we played in a few bands together. After a while we all realized that it was fun to play with different musicians from time to time. The musicians I enjoyed playing with the most were also some of my dearest friends, so we stuck together for many years.

Robert Beddoe was one of my best friends, and a very talented bass guitar player. I was blessed to know him in his short life. We played together in many bands, and I was the man behind the drums from junior high school into our late twenties. The music was tight, and the friendship grew.

Our friendship started on the first day of junior high school, when I noticed him tapping his foot to a rhythm I thought I knew, and asked, "Is the song you are tapping to Purple Haze?"

He replied, "Yes, how did you know?"

I answered, "I play the drums, and that's an easy one."

"What's your name?" he asked.

"Bob," I replied with a grin. "And yours is too."

He did a double-take and asked, "How did you know that?"

"We're in science class together. I heard your name called when the teacher was taking attendance. Are you in a band?"

"No, but I'd like to start one," he replied. "I play bass guitar."

He asked me if I wanted to go to his house on Saturday and bring my drums. I told him I didn't have a car or a driver's license, but I was sure my mother would bring me over. We flashed each other a peace sign, and so began our long, friendly, and respectful relationship.

When I got home from school that day, I rushed into my house with exciting news. "Mom, Mom, guess what?"

She asked me, "What's all the excitement about?"

"I met a guy today in school that plays the bass guitar and wants to start a band! Can you drive me and my drums to his house on

Saturday? He wants to jam with me!"

I could see that she was happy for me and with a big smile said, "I think that would be a wonderful thing for you to do."

When Saturday came, I loaded my drums into the back seat of my mother's car and she drove me to Bob's house. That was the beginning of our playing together, which lasted nearly twenty years. The music was cool, and the fun we had was priceless.

Bob was a unique person. He was the only bass player I'd ever seen take a right-handed bass guitar, flip it around to the left, and used it as a left-handed bass guitar. He didn't even change the strings around, as a left-handed bass player normally would, but played it as it was. The only other musician that I'd heard of being known for doing this was Jimi Hendrix, who would use a right-handed guitar flipped around to use left-handed.

During the years that we played in bands together, some of the best times we had were when we would stay up half the night, thinking up names for the band we started. The laughs were endless.

Bob also had an affinity for flying and explored the world of gliders. Eventually he took up hang-gliding. In many ways he resembled a bird, with his long legs and quirky bird-like movements.

His talents allowed him to branch out into much more than being the bass man who kept us all in time. He opened a very successful custom picture framing business that he ran in his home. Before there were the big stores that offered this type of service, Robert's framing shop was one of the only places you could have that type of custom work done in our area.

Another thing he enjoyed was restoring older foreign cars. His parents were divorced when he was around ten, and he lived with his mother and sister, not far from me. From time to time he would go to visit his father, who lived in a small town in the Berkshire

Mountains of Massachusetts. His father also was into European auto restoration. It was one of the things that they enjoyed doing together.

I'd always wanted an old-style 1950s Jaguar. Once I knew that Beddoe had similar interests when it came to old foreign cars, I asked him, "Bob, if I could find an old Jag cheap, that needs to be restored, will you help me restore it?"

"Yes, of course I will." He further added, "You can park it at my house until we have time to work on it."

A few weeks later I located and purchased a 1959 Jaguar MK III, with left-hand drive, painted white, which we planned to restore together. Being the auto restoration guru, he was going to be my teacher during our project, which would one day produce a fun, fine British ride. We would share another great thing. I had the car brought over to his house on a flatbed, and parked it next to his garage, where it would be safe, waiting for our project to begin.

By this time I had ten years of learning the business of piano restoration and sales and had recently been advised to start getting serious about dealing primarily with Steinway pianos. Beddoe wanted to be involved in this, too.

The living room in his home, where he also ran his picture framing business, was a perfect place to display Steinway pianos. We both agreed that we would enjoy being involved in each other's projects. We also continued playing music together, as we had been doing for close to twenty years. The stage was set, and on it were a bass and drums, an old Jaguar, and soon to come, some Steinway grands.

Thanks to my mother's vast experience and her knowledge of nationwide advertising networks, I was able to place my "Steinway Wanted" ads all over the country. She guided me with the information I would use to start my nationwide hunt. Once the phone started to ring with Steinway owners who were ready to sell, I prepared myself for what was to be the start of my lifelong career.

I started my first advertising campaign in New York State, since I was already there. Most of the newspapers I advertised in were the dailies. That way, the readers would see the ad running continuously. I placed the same ad to run for two weeks at a time, hoping that if a Steinway owner who was considering selling their piano viewed it many times, it would sink in enough to get them to pick up the phone and call me.

After the first three days of my ads running, I received a call from a nice older man who wanted to sell his Steinway grand, located in Syracuse. I asked him for some details about his piano, but all he knew was that his late wife had purchased it from a local church more than forty years before we spoke and played it as often as she could, until her passing a few years previously. He also told me that it had originally been a player-grand piano, but all of the player parts had been removed prior to them purchasing it. After speaking with him and hearing the history of his wife and her love for that piano, I was ready to go see the Steinway and hopefully buy it.

At the time my first hunt began, I was partnered with another good friend and musician, Rob, a well-known guitarist from Wappinger's Falls, New York. I'd played in a few local bands with him during my early years. Since Rob and I were part of the local music scene, we knew many of the same people, and Bob Beddoe was one of them.

Rob and I also had a lot in common when it came to our love of pianos. Rob owned a Steinway upright piano that his father had just purchased for him as a birthday gift. Since I was experienced in moving pianos, Rob and his father asked me if I would help move the piano from the store in New York City where they purchased it to their home. I was glad to help.

Rob's father, Ed, was a classical pianist who owned a restored

Steinway 7-foot model B grand piano. I always marveled at the love he displayed while playing his instrument. Rob also enjoyed playing his father's Steinway.

Shortly after we decided to take a shot at doing business together, Rob lost his father to cancer. After Ed's passing, Rob and his mother, Marie, asked me if I could help them sell his father's Steinway grand, which I did. It was the first Steinway grand I'd ever sold.

The day before Rob and I were to take our trip to Syracuse for the first Steinway grand I would buy, I rented a small U-Haul truck. We tossed in the collection of old blankets that I'd been using for years to move pianos locally, a box of old rope, and a piano dolly.

Our plan was to get on the road early the next day, so we could drive to Syracuse and be back in the same day. I gave Rob a call about 7 a.m. and told him I would pick him up around 8:30. I arrived at his house near that time. We were ready to hit the road.

Just as we were about to close his basement door and walk to the truck, Rob's mother called out to him from upstairs and told him he had a phone call. Rob walked back inside to answer it. It was another guitarist friend, Ed, who was in a band with Bob Beddoe at the time. Ed gave Rob the most terrible news we could imagine.

Bob had been killed early that day while flying his ultra-light plane. Rob came back downstairs and told me the news. I was never so shaken. On the day I was going to leave on my very first Steinway hunt, one of my very best friends had lost his life. Devastated, I tried to make sense of what I had just heard. I needed to decide whether to continue with my plan to go ahead with the trip or cancel it. Rob and I sat in the truck, silent for a long time.

As bad as we both felt about the loss of our friend, we decided to go forward with our trip that day, knowing that when we returned, nothing would be any different from what we knew had taken place.

With heavy hearts, we started our trip.

We made it to Syracuse in record time, had a short visit with the old gentleman, and bought the Steinway that his wife had loved to play. It was a 6'3" ebony model OR that was in fairly good playing shape, not too bad-looking, and in its original condition, except for the player parts that had been removed. We packed it in the truck and headed for home.

With Bob Beddoe gone, the plans we had were not going to happen. The old Jaguar got sold for parts, and of course the plan to fix and sell Steinways from his home was over. I keep memories of the great music we played as teens and into our twenties close in my heart.

As the years went on, I opened a few small piano shops where I would refurbish, rebuild, and wholesale Steinways to the public and other dealers. I have been doing so for almost fifty years now, but I will never forget the pain I felt on the day the big Steinway hunt began . . . the day I lost a best friend.

Chapter 5

THANKS FROM 35,000 FEET

As I write this story, I'm flying at 35,000 feet with my dear wife, Ronnie, on a Friday, the start of Memorial Day weekend in 2015. We are traveling to Las Vegas for a little fun and relaxation. This flight reminded me of the conversation that I'd had with a gentleman named Robert Paine while he was at 35,000 feet.

Early in my career, when I was dealing strictly with Steinways, I would strive to match the pianist to the Steinway pianos I found. Before I'd offer a piano to a dealer at wholesale, I advertised the piano in the *New York Times*. I'd get many serious pianists who would hop on a train from Grand Central Station, or drive from wherever they lived in the Greater New York area, to Hyde Park, New York, where I displayed them in my home. Since I didn't have the overhead of a large store or piano shop, I was able to advertise my pianos at lower prices than other piano dealers, which was very enticing to buyers.

The piano I advertised this time was an 1878 ebony 85-note Steinway model B. Mr. Paine called on a Friday, very interested in the piano, so we set up a time for him to view the Steinway on Saturday morning.

He drove up to the house, got out of his car, and I met him at the front door. In many ways he resembled my father, who had passed away eighteen years before.

We talked about Steinways for quite some time. He loved these pianos, as I did. When he sat down and played the Steinway B, I saw that he was a fine pianist and I was amazed that his technique was identical to my late father's. I listened and enjoyed his playing. I felt as though my father, who I missed so badly, was in the room.

After he performed Rachmaninoff's Prelude in G Minor, which was my father's favorite piece to perform, he got up and told me that he liked the piano very much, but would prefer an 88-note modern scale Steinway B.

We got along as though we had known each other for many years. He asked me if I could find him an early turn-of-the-century 1900's Victorian model B, in original condition, that I could restore for him. I told him that I could, and we shook on it. Mr. Paine was in search of his dream Steinway and I was determined to find it for him.

Remarkably, within a few days I received a call from a person who wanted to sell the identical piano that Bob Paine had asked me to find. It was outside of the Boston area, and they were anxious to sell it. They were moving and couldn't take it with them, since they were downsizing.

It was winter and snowing, so the trip to see, hopefully buy, and move this gem was tricky. Nevertheless, I made the trip and successfully purchased it.

It was a real beauty; an ebony 1904 Steinway model B, 6' 10.5" with "ice cream cone" legs, a scalloped music rack, and a pedal-lyre in the shape of King David's lyre. This was Steinway's most favored Victorian-style grand. It was just what Mr. Paine had ordered. I was satisfied, knowing that I was about to fulfill his wishes.

I called Bob to tell him the good news about the Steinway. He was so thrilled that he asked me if I would drive the piano to his house, so he could play it. I explained to him that it wasn't in playable condition. It needed complete restoration. He didn't care; he just wanted to see it in the back of the truck.

I liked this guy a lot, so I drove to his home in Pleasantville, New York, the day after returning from Boston with the piano. I attempted his steep driveway, covered in snow and ice, three times before I successfully made it up. He met me outside. Although it was cold and snowy, he had a dream and I wanted to see it fulfilled.

He hopped up into the back of the truck and I, along with my helper, set up the piano there for his inspection. Bob sat down on the piano stool and played that old Steinway in near zero-degree weather for what seemed like an eternity but was actually only about twenty minutes. It was obvious that he fell in love with it just as it was.

He was so thrilled that I'd found the exact Steinway he wanted that he offered to do some very extensive research for me regarding Steinways. He thought it would be helpful to expand my calling: hunting Steinways. Aside from being a professor of piano at Pace University, Bob was an upper-level executive for the Nielsen Research Company. He had access to many of the facts and figures concerning the volume of Steinway grands manufactured in all years, and all models and sizes.

I soon introduced him to the owners of one of the most highly skilled and well-recognized piano restoration shops in the New York

City area. They specialized in complete restorations of Steinways, and he agreed to have his piano restored there. This was to be a six-month project that after completion would produce an instrument that met all of his expectations.

During the time his Steinway was in restoration, I received a call from Bob. The voice on the other end of the phone said, "Hello Robert, this is Bob Paine calling from 35,000 feet."

I smiled and answered, "Hi Bob. How are things with you?"

He responded, "Very good. I just wanted to let you know that I've completed my research on the number of available Steinway grand pianos manufactured from 1900 to date."

I was impressed and told him, "That's great news!"

He told me that with the volume of used Steinway grands that sold new, and continued to sell used each year, he thought there would be more than enough available for me to base my wholesale business model on. I could, if I was very diligent and continued my search full-time, be successful in this business. He added that when he returned home from his business trip to Chicago, he would mail me all the information that he had collected for me, so that I would have it for future use. This was a very helpful, priceless, and kind gift he was giving me for finding his dream piano.

Now, many years later, I am still grateful to Bob for giving me the knowledge that encouraged me to pursue what became my life's work. In return, I am proud to thank him in this story, written at 35,000 feet. It exemplifies an adage we all know: "The sky's the limit."

Chapter 6

BURNED OUT IN BUFFALO

As the twilight of an early winter's evening was settling in, I received a call from the owner of a demolition company in Buffalo, New York. The man's voice sounded old and tough. He told me of an 1880s stone church that had burned in a wicked fire. The only things that were left standing were the stone foundation, the outer stone walls, a few broken stained-glass windows, a few caved-in sections of floor, and in the basement, a black Victorian Steinway grand piano.

First, he asked me if I was interested. I asked him the condition of the piano, and he told me all that was left was the outer rim, the plate (or harp), some of the keys, and that it was still standing on its legs. The rest of the piano had burned. No top, no music rack or desk, and no key cover.

I wasn't sure what to expect, but I figured that if I was to get this piano, I'd better speak up. I made him an offer sight unseen, and he accepted quickly. He firmly told me that if I did not haul it out of the church by sunset the very next day, he was going to crush it along with the remains of the church at sunrise the following day. He had a deadline that needed to be kept.

Buffalo was a six-hour drive from my home in Poughkeepsie, New York. If I was to save this Steinway, I needed to be in the truck at dawn the next morning. If I didn't go, the Steinway was doomed. However, this piano sounded like one I could buy low and either restore myself or sell to someone who could. The only way I would know, was to see it.

I was on the road by 10 a.m. The temperature was nearly 40 when I left, so I dressed in a T-shirt, sweats, and a lightweight windbreaker. I figured I'd be okay, since I'd be driving in a heated truck. I planned to load quickly and return the same day.

Since the speed limit was 55 mph, it was a long, slow drive. It was also a dark, dreary, damp day. After almost six hours of driving with a few stops for gas and food, as the sun was just starting to set, I finally reached my destination.

I got out of my truck and stood in front of the skeleton of a giant old three-story stone church.

There I met the owner of the demolition company and his crew of three men. He explained to me that we didn't have much time to load the piano out of the church. The sun would be setting soon, and there was no electricity. He did have flashlights, but that wasn't much light to guide me.

He walked me into what was left of the structure. I was amazed that the outside stone walls were still standing, along with a few badly damaged stained-glass windows. The floors were mostly gone. The only thing that was still inside, standing on its legs in the basement, was the Steinway grand.

He lowered me down to the basement with a large rope tied to his truck's rear bumper so I could inspect the piano. There, I stood in a few inches of ice-cold water, with an ebony 1880s model A1, 6'2" Victorian grand piano with fireplug-designed legs, so named because they resembled a fire hydrant. It had barely made it through the fire that had destroyed everything else around it.

The A1 was the flagship piano that all Steinways from that day forward were modeled after. The designs that were first used in this piano were the duplex scale for stringing, as well as the tubular action frame that was used to hold all the moving parts that controlled the hammers, which struck the strings to create the sound.

I made the deal with him as previously agreed, and he offered to help me haul the piano out. He pulled me back up with the rope, and I went to my truck to get my piano skid, straps, blankets, and tools. Back inside, again he lowered me to the basement, along with my moving equipment.

There was no roof on the church, no floors, no top on the piano, and no soundboard because it all had burned. I was lying under the piano unscrewing the legs and pedals, on my back in the icy water, regretting that I hadn't prepared better, or dressed more appropriately. I looked up through the piano, past the first floor, past the second and third floors, and out through the roof at the twilight sky, terrified that at any moment, the skeleton of the building could collapse and trap me underneath this piano. The stars twinkled as light snow fell into my eyes.

My shirt and pants were soaking wet, and I was freezing cold, but in my complete exhilaration I realized that it was my fate to be there, and to be the one who saved the Steinway. I packed up the piano, on its side, on a moving skid, wrapped it with blankets, and the demo crew helped me hoist it up to the first floor. They helped me load it into my truck, we all shook hands, and away I drove, cold, wet, and completely satisfied.

I cranked up the heat all the way and drove the six-plus hours home.

Late in the afternoon the next day, exhausted from the night before, I drove the piano to my shop. My helper and I took it out of the truck and did our best to set it up in a standing position. Now, in better light, I could really examine the piano. In its silence, unable to be played, it seemed to yearn to survive. I was told that the piano was in that church from the time it was new. I could only imagine some of the rousing hymns that had been performed on this piano. I made the decision to restore it to its original glory, but first it had to be taken apart.

At the time, I was working with a few Steinway restoration experts who traveled up from New York City on weekends to my shop in Kingston, New York. They told me that considering the piano's horrible condition, it would take a lot of work to restore and would be very costly. I was willing to do and spend what I needed to, for this piano to have life again.

The challenge was on. Out came the keyboard, off went the strings that hadn't popped off by themselves from the heat of the fire. The piano still held the scent from the fire that ravaged it. I removed the bent and badly burned damper heads—the felt wedges that would stop the strings from resonating.

The piano was ready to be shipped to a well-known restoration facility in Astoria, Queens. It had been manufactured in Astoria, and just a little over 100 years later, it was returned to a restoration shop in that neighborhood. There it would be restored by a man who for many years had worked at the Steinway factory, and his son. It was to have all the missing parts replaced and the remaining case parts repaired, a new top made, the cabinet refinished in black satin lacquer, and a new soundboard, pin block, and strings installed.

Once the piano was received by the restoration shop, I received a call from the owner. He told me that it was, by far, in the worst shape of any Steinway he had ever seen. He also couldn't assure me that after the work was complete, the piano would have the correct tone and sustain it should have. Since the wooden rim had been so badly dried out from the fire, it might not be able to be sealed properly once he stripped off the remaining lacquer. I was committed to having the piano restored, since I had developed a special connection to it, so I gave him the go-ahead to do the work, and I would take responsibility for the outcome.

During the seven-month wait for the piano to be completed, I had more than enough time to restore the keyboard and hammer action. I ordered a new set of high-quality, off-white key-tops. Most of the ivory, which had covered the keys from the time it was manufactured, was cracked and chipped, if not missing. I enjoyed re-covering the keys. It was the one procedure involved in piano restoration that I trained myself to do in my early years, while restoring mostly off-brand pianos. I did this work by hand, using a one-edge blade and a file. I'd learned most of the other procedures involved in piano restoration from the old masters, but this I had taught myself.

The first time I attempted to pull off an old set of badly damaged ivory keys, I paid dearly. It was in the late 1970s during an electrical blackout. It was nearing dusk, so I had to light several candles to give me some light, but it wasn't enough. I cut my hands many times. By the time I had removed all of the old ivory, the wooden keys were bloodstained and the candles nearly burned out, but the keys were ready to be re-covered. It wasn't a surprise to most people who knew me then to see my hands covered with cuts and Band-Aids.

Today, there are machines that do this work, but some of us still prefer to do it by hand. I prefer hand tools over power tools. To me, it's much more satisfying to hold the key in your hand, as you feel your way to the finished product, rather than need to depend on an automated device. I am a purist when it comes to that type of work.

Shortly into the seventh month of the restoration, I received a call from the shop with the news that the piano was ready. I drove to Queens to inspect it. The 1880s Steinway had turned out better than I had hoped.

Standing proud, it now looked almost new. It had a new lid, keyboard cover, music rack, and desk, completely refinished in satin black, with a new soundboard, tuning pin block, and strings. The Steinway was ready to be brought back to my shop to complete the assembly.

Once back in my shop, the restored keyboard and hammer action were placed into the piano. After more than three weeks of stretching the strings to bring it up to concert pitch, the piano was finely tuned, producing the rich, lush tone that Steinways are famous for. It was ready to play. My staff and I rolled it from our work area into the showroom.

I advertised the piano for sale in the *New York Times*. I priced it much lower than any of the other Steinways for sale. If a serious piano buyer was to travel from New York City, approximately an hour and a half to my shop, the price needed to be enticing enough to get their attention, and it did. I received many calls, but one woman in particular wanted to bring her teenage daughter to play it as soon as possible. She had been playing on a small electric keyboard and needed to upgrade to a real piano. If her daughter liked it, she would buy it for her. I went into my showroom and tuned it, hoping this would be the last tuning while in my care. I had saved this Steinway on the night before it was to be buried within the remains of the building where it was last played. It was time for the resurrected instrument to go into the hands of its next owner.

The woman and her daughter pulled up to my shop around noon the next day. I greeted them and led them to the piano.

"Oh, it's beautiful," the mother exclaimed when she first saw the piano.

The daughter asked, "May I play it?"

I replied, "Of course. Please do."

The girl sat down to the piano and began to play. She played her favorite classical pieces, beginning with Beethoven's "Für Elise," and continuing with his "Moonlight" Sonata. Her mother was smiling, seeing her daughter enjoying the rich tones. The woman asked a few questions about the restoration process. I explained to her all the work that had been done on the piano. Since it had been completely rebuilt, and was magnificent in every way, I didn't feel that it was necessary to tell her how I had acquired the piano or of its history. I would have told her if she'd asked, but she didn't.

Her daughter liked the piano and wanted it. Although my asking price was very fair, she asked for a better deal. I wasn't going to let it go too much lower. I'd invested so much time and money into restoring this Steinway, that I'd almost lost track of the real numbers. I was very close to break-even when I made her one last offer, and she accepted it. We made a plan for payment and delivery, and they left.

I walked over to the piano, stared at the keyboard, and played a few notes. In my mind I reminisced about the day that I'd first seen this piano and marveled about how far it had come. I imagined the days when this piano was the instrument that filled the church with beautiful music; that had accompanied hymns for the many people who had enjoyed it for over a century. This piano, with my assistance, found its way back to the place of its birth, to be restored by the students of the master craftsmen who had originally created it. It was now going into the hands of a young woman who would cherish it.

Chapter 7

FROM MONK TO MASTER

In the early days of my hunting for Steinways, a call came in from a Deacon Monk at a monastery in Newport, Rhode Island. He told me they had acquired an 1800s rosewood carved Steinway concert grand through a recent donation.

He explained that it was much too big for them to keep. They were interested in selling it to raise money to purchase plants from a local nursery for the main chapel. He also told me that he had received the history of the piano from the Steinway factory only weeks before. The piano was dated 1898, and was manufactured in Hamburg, Germany.

At that point my interest was piqued. The reason that this piano appealed to me was that it was a German Steinway. Most of the Steinway pianos that I was used to seeing were manufactured in New York. It was a rare find to encounter a Hamburg. I made an appointment with him to inspect the piano.

Two days later I got in my truck with a helper, my moving

equipment, and a pocket full of cash, anticipating the purchase of this Steinway.

That trip took more than six hours on a day when the snow was falling steadily. If the weather had been better, it would have taken less than four hours.

Slowly and steadily, I drove through the snow to Rhode Island to view this old gem. Once we arrived, we were greeted by the Deacon, who led us to the piano.

Much to my surprise, this 1800s Hamburg Steinway concert grand in rosewood looked like a new piano. I was confused because I had assumed I was going to see an old Steinway in need of restoration. Instead, this magnificent Steinway had already been restored. The Deacon explained to me that from the records he received, this piano had been completely restored at the Steinway factory a short time before it was donated to them, three years previously.

I asked, "How much are you asking for the piano?"

His reply was, "Just enough to pay the nursery for the new plants we want to buy for the main chapel."

If I purchased the piano, my greens would pay for their greens!

I agreed to his asking price, and we shook on it. Then he showed me the route that I would have to take to move the piano out of the building. It was going to be an extremely difficult task, especially for only two people. There was a long hallway, with three double stair landings. We needed to take the piano down six steps, across a landing that was shorter than the piano, then up six steps to a plateau. Each time the piano reached the lower landing, we needed to use two dollies, see-sawing the piano on them to reach the top of the next set of steps. There were three sets like this, so it would have to be done three times before we would reach the door to take the piano to the truck.

I hesitated, trying to decide if the piano was worth all of the effort it was going to take to remove it. He offered, "If you think that the move is too difficult, and you don't want to buy the piano, it's okay. I have someone coming from Boston in an hour who will take it."

That decided it. I paid him for the piano, brought in my moving gear, and started the process of getting the precious beast to the truck.

It was the most difficult piano move I have ever encountered, moving the largest and heaviest Steinway grand the company had ever made. After the piano was safely in the truck, I headed home.

The next day I brought the piano into my shop. After a full inspection of this magnificent piece of musical art, I decided I wouldn't wholesale it to a dealer, as I did most of the Steinways I hunted. I would offer it to the public for sale instead.

I listed it for sale in my local shopper, *The Pennysaver*. A few days later, a woman called. She said she was very interested in it. I made an appointment to show the piano to her and her husband in the early afternoon of the next day.

When they arrived, they introduced themselves as Mr. and Mrs. Robert Boyle. We chatted about the piano at first. He said that he was a writer for *Sports Illustrated*, and also founder and president of Riverkeeper, an environmental action group committed to cleaning up the Hudson River.

Robert was concerned that the piano was too large for any of the rooms in their house, but would fit perfectly in the large entryway of their home on the Hudson in Cold Spring, New York. He said that if I could get it delivered to the house by Saturday, and make sure it was also concert tuned, he would make me a fair offer. That was four days away; I was sure I could deliver it in time.

I was curious, so I asked him, "Why is it so imperative that the Steinway be in your home and concert tuned by Saturday?"

He smiled and said, "We're hosting a gala affair Saturday evening. We're entertaining many of our friends, colleagues, and dignitaries, including Robert F. Kennedy Jr. Vladimir Horowitz is going to perform."

I was awestruck that the great Steinway concert pianist Vladimir Horowitz was going to be playing this piano.

We agreed on a price, and I delivered the piano the next day. It received a concert tuning that Friday, and the Steinway was ready in time for the master to perform on it.

Robert had invited me to the gala, but I had my next Steinway buying trip already planned, so I had to decline. I later regretted not postponing my trip, but my show also had to go on.

Chapter 8

AMSTERDAM FIREMAN

One Steinway that needs to have its story told will never get the chance to sing again. Known as the Steinway Square Grand Piano, it is made of Brazilian rosewood with Rococo cabinet styling. First introduced to the marketplace in 1856, it was manufactured up until 1889. There were only two changes to its string scale design for the entire time it was made. The single most important change to the string scale was introduced in the final years of its production. Instead of having a two-string unison from the beginning of the tenor section all the way to the top end of the treble section, the new scale would now have a three-string unison, very similar to the modern Steinway. These newer design Steinway Square Grands were much fuller-sounding instruments than the earlier ones, and therefore they were much more desirable.

The Steinway Square Grand in this story was one of the great ones. It was located at the farthest north point of New York state, in a small town called Massena. A middle-aged woman with two teenage girls had purchased it from one of her neighbors, whose elderly father had owned it for over 90 years. The neighbor's father had passed away, and the neighbor sold it to her. She was planning to have it restored, but decided it was a costlier project than she wanted to invest in.

She contacted me from an ad I was running in her local newspaper. She managed to find the serial number on the bottom of one of the legs, which I researched with Steinway in New York. I discovered that it was manufactured in the last production year of that piano's design. I was very intrigued by having a chance to own this very rare and special Steinway.

Two days after my research with Steinway in New York City, I contacted the owner and we agreed on a price, contingent on whether the piano was in good enough condition for restoration. This was one that I wanted to restore.

As had happened many times before, I was about to be driving in a snowstorm. I called up my best friend, Dave, to see if he was up for a long, slippery ride. Dave and I made very few Steinway hunting trips together. Most of my trips were far away from New York, and he was employed locally, so it was hard for us to arrange unless I was hunting fairly locally. It just happened that our timing was right on this one. He usually didn't say no to a good time, and he was always up for a new and exciting adventure. We were born in the same town and were lifelong friends who regularly played musical instruments together, primarily guitars. We also worked on pianos together. We had a love and respect for each other like brothers of different mothers, from the time we met in 1971 until his sad passing in 2013. Dave's kindness and his humor live on in the lives of the people he touched.

Dave and I got a very late start, around 9 the next evening, due to the snow falling all day. It was very hard to drive until the roads were clear enough to travel. We headed due north up the New York State Thruway.

After driving almost three hours from the New Paltz entrance, we reached the exit for Amsterdam, New York, which is one exit past Albany. We decided to stay in Amsterdam and rest for the night, so we grabbed a cheap hotel next to a run-down bar.

The bar looked like it was about to close when we walked in. It was nearly empty, with not much going on that late and snowy night. The bartender said we could double up if we wanted because he was closing real soon. Instead, we tripled up, each chugging down three vodka and limes. We stumbled back to our room, laughing and joking all the way.

When we got back to the room, we both crashed on our beds, clothes on, lights on. After a while, we both got up and started joking around again.

On a small dresser there was an old microwave oven. I said to Dave, "What do you think would happen if we put the phone book in the oven and cooked it for a few minutes?" He replied, "Can't say Laddie, never cooked one before!" Dave often called me Laddie, since he had five years on me. After some more joking around, I laid back on my bed and fell asleep again, still clothed.

I woke up to the sound of the microwave door blasting open, a flaming phone book hurling across the room. We both jumped up out of our beds and started stamping out the yellow pages of the Albany directory.

I screamed at Dave, "What the hell were you thinking?" He replied, "You asked me if I'd ever cooked a phone book. I didn't think it would catch on fire."

Luckily for us, there was no damage to the oven or the room. We both passed out until the sun came up.

The next morning, we got into my truck and up the highway. We were hungry for food, and a Steinway. After five hours of driving, all the while cracking jokes, Dave and I were finally close to our destination. Once we reached the home, we pulled up and were greeted by the owner and her two daughters. The woman walked us to the garage, where the piano was tightly wrapped in blankets on its side, resting on a concrete floor. Dave and I managed to lift one end and dolly it outside, so we could take a look at its condition in better light. The garage was very dark, and the sun was not much brighter above the cloudy winter sky.

We inspected the Steinway, making sure it was stored properly and was a worthy candidate for restoration. All the original parts were there, and it was in decent shape; a true musical time traveler.

We made an agreement with the owner to buy it. Deciding to partner on the deal, Dave bought the piano, and I was to pay for the replacement of the action parts.

The owner was very happy that it was going to be restored, as she had once planned to do, and we were glad to do it. We loaded up the piano and headed for home. Seven hours later, we were tired from driving and our faces hurt from laughing, but we had made it back with our prize.

A few days after we returned home, Dave and I unpacked the Steinway. We took it to my small shop and disassembled most of it. We agreed to hire a known furniture refinisher in Ulster County, New York, for that part of the restoration, and delivered the piano to him.

Dave and I planned to restore the hammer action and restring the piano. We put off our end of the work, because we knew the case finishing was going to take three or so months.

The refinisher called us at the end of the third week to let us know that the legs and top of the piano would be ready for pickup the following Monday. We thought that those piano parts would be better kept in our hands than to be lying around a busy furniture refinishing shop, so we went to get them. We also made a sizable payment to him.

To our surprise, the refinisher called in the middle of the second month and said he would have the piano completed in one week. We had planned our payment schedule around a three- to four-month finish date. We were happy he was moving quickly, but it was going too fast for us to make our final payment that early. He had refinished many pianos for me previously, and I figured we would be okay keeping our agreement for payment as it was. I called to let him know that the early work was appreciated, but we could not get the final payment to him for at least three more weeks.

The man went crazy on the phone. He started cursing and screaming, and threatened to drag the piano outside, using a tow chain with his pickup truck, and burn it in his driveway if I did not come by with the cash by Friday of the following week.

I told him he was nuts and if he did it, he would end up in court and would regret it. He repeated that it was going to happen if I didn't show up by Friday of the next week. I laughed and told him to hang on to the piano until we showed up in a few weeks with the money. Then I hung up the phone.

A few weeks went by, and we saved up the money to get the piano away from this nut.

I called him and asked him when a good time was to pick up the piano. He said, "I dragged it out of my shop with a chain like I told you I would and burned it." I said to him, "Do you know how much trouble you are in?" He said to leave him alone and not bother him anymore.

I was completely stunned. I could not believe what he had just told me on the phone. He had deliberately destroyed one of the rarest Steinway pianos on the planet.

Since Dave had ownership of the piano, he was the one who had to file a claim against the refinisher for the loss of it.

We drove together to the county courthouse, and Dave filed a claim against the refinisher, stating exactly what had been told to me over the phone about what the refinisher did to the Steinway. After a few weeks, Dave received a letter from the court with a date for us to appear to claim our losses for this atrocity.

As I recall, the court appearance was around 6 p.m. on a weeknight. We pulled up, expecting a rude greeting from the refinisher. Instead, he was very quiet and slouched in his seat a few rows ahead of us. There were two or three cases before ours, so it gave us time to prepare. It was coming close to the moment when the story of this piano, now in piano heaven, would be told.

The defendant in this case was called, as the judge read out our claim. "Mr. X, the plaintiff, Mr. Dave Gene Senk, claims that his partner, Bob Friedman, called you to pick up his piano from your shop as agreed, on a date that was within the time frame he had been given by you to pay and remove his piano from your shop. You told him that his piano was taken outside by you and burned. Is this true?" the judge asked. The man answered, "Yes."

The judge asked him, "What exactly did you do to this piano?" The man said, "I wrapped a chain around it, dragged it out into my driveway, and burned it." You could see the look of complete surprise on the face of the judge. He asked the accused, "Why would you burn something that did not belong to you?" His answer was that we owed him money for the work, and he wanted to get paid. The judge replied, "Now you will not get paid, and you will also have to pay for the piano that you destroyed."

We won the case but received nowhere near what the Steinway would have been worth if it had been completely restored. Since the refinisher lived locally, and the judge was a strong influence in that community, I hoped the word got out, so that people would stay far away from that piano killer.

A few weeks later, I took the large part of this piano's top, attached the four legs underneath it, and made it into my first office desk. The other part of the top I affixed to the wall behind the desk and used it as a matching shelf; a real Steinway office ensemble in Brazilian rosewood, no less.

Chapter 9

THE LADY'S FRIEND MUST STAY

The reasons that most owners contacted me to sell their Steinways were that they were downsizing, needed the money, or were no longer playing the piano. Sometimes there were unique circumstances that called for me to understand the seller's passion, beyond just the sale.

In 1992, I received a call from Loretta Duncan, a retired piano professor living in Gallatin, Tennessee. Gallatin is located approximately 30 miles northeast of Nashville, the "Country Music Capital of the World." Our conversation about her career, her Steinway, and her life lasted for over an hour. I knew from this phone call that I would need to put plenty of time aside to visit with her. I'd have to help her find a comfort zone in which she could be completely sure before she would sell me her Steinway.

This was the first time I'd advertised to buy Steinways in her area. I knew that many famous, and hopeful, musicians lived in the Nashville area, so it made sense to try my luck at hunting there. Shortly after our first phone call, I scheduled a trip to meet with her, as well as five other people who wanted to sell their Steinways.

Once I was in Nashville, I gave her a call. It was late in the afternoon. I asked her, "Is it okay to visit you now, so close to dinner time?" "Yes," she replied. "If you have time, I'd like you to stay and have a bite to eat with me. Would that work for you?"

I was hungry, so that sounded good. I responded, "After everything you told me about your life, I'd like very much to visit with you, and over dinner would be a great way to talk music and pianos."

I proceeded to drive to her house.

I was as excited to meet her as I was to see her piano. From the moment she opened her front door to greet me, we started to chat as if we'd known each other for years. The first thing I did was give her my business card. I sensed from our phone conversations that just in case we didn't decide on the piano sale that day, she should have a way to reach me once my local advertising ended.

Her house was small, and her walnut Steinway, model M grand, 5'7", took up a large part of her living room and a corner of her dining room. In my experience, when someone gave up that much space in their home for a grand piano, music was one of the most important things in their life, if not the most important. As we talked, she described all the moves she had made throughout her life to keep her close to her piano music, and to the life she loved.

She was a graduate of Juilliard School of Music in New York City, with a master's degree in piano composition. Loretta explained, "I never had a plan to be a performance major, even though I performed many times. I even performed at Carnegie Hall during a piano competition, while attending Juilliard."

I asked her, "How did you do at the competition?"

She smiled and said, "I did very well."

I asked her how she ended up in the Nashville area. She explained, "My late husband was offered a transfer with the company he was working for at the time, and we both agreed that it would be a good move. Our son and daughter were both married, with children of their own, so it made the move much easier. In addition, I was offered a position to teach piano composition in a local university, as I had been doing in New York, so we would both have steady incomes after we relocated."

During our conversation, we enjoyed a healthful dinner made up of a salad with raspberry vinaigrette followed by a main course of spinach penne with a light pesto sauce.

We went back into her living room after dinner, and she told me the real reasons why she wanted to sell her piano.

"I'm eighty-five years old, I have arthritis in both of my hands, and find it difficult to play my Steinway. I'm also planning to sell my house and move into much smaller living quarters. However, I'm sad that the piano can't go with me."

I asked her if she ever sat down and played. She told me that every now and then, she'd play what she could. I felt bad for her; music and her piano were such a huge part of her life, and I was about to take that away from her.

I asked her, "Would you mind playing the piano for me, so I could hear what it sounds like from a distance?" She got up from her easy chair and walked slowly over to the piano, placed both of her hands over the keys, and pushed them down lightly, just for a moment, hard enough for the hammers to strike the strings, so I could hear it. Then she stopped, and with a sad look on her face, walked back to sit in her chair.

"Does it sound good to you, Bob?" she asked.

I replied, "It has a sweet tone, like the lady who plays it."

"Do you want to buy it?" she asked.

"I would, but I don't want to take away your music."

The respect that I had for this woman after hearing how hard and long she worked on her career in music, and the love she had for her piano, helped me decide for us both that it was not yet time for her to part with her piano.

I told her my thoughts and that I'd like to buy it, but not now, while she still had an interest in playing it.

"Would you consider buying it at a later date, when I'm ready to move?" she asked.

I said, "Of course I will."

We planned to stay in touch, and she said that when the day came that she was ready to part with her beloved Steinway, she'd contact me.

As she walked me to the door, I thanked her for the tasty dinner and the stories about her long, successful music career. I drove away in my truck, not knowing if I'd ever hear from her again.

In 1996, while I was working in Yonkers, New York, at the Piano Cooperative, I received a call from a woman who introduced herself as Corinne Masters, Loretta Duncan's daughter. She told me that she spoke with her mother many times about my visit to see her piano. Loretta also told her daughter that she'd taped my business card on her refrigerator, and once the day came to sell her Steinway, to call me.

I asked her how her mother was doing. She told me that sadly, her mother had passed away a few months earlier. Corinne asked me if I was still interested in purchasing the Steinway. I told Corinne, "I'm happy to know that your mother kept her piano for the remainder of her life, and kept her promise to offer it to me when the time came."

I told Corinne that I wanted to buy it, and that I could send a mover with the money to her mother's home to pick it up as soon as she was ready to have it moved out. She told me, "My mother would be extremely happy knowing you were the one that ended up buying her piano."

Since I was busy managing a piano restoration shop, I was not available to drive all the way from New York to Tennessee and back. I asked my oldest son, Michael, who was working with me part-time, if he wanted the job.

He said, "Dad, you rent the truck and I'll find a friend to go with me." So, I did.

The next day we loaded piano-moving equipment into the truck, and they headed to Tennessee.

Her house was 895 miles from Yonkers one way, a little under 1,800 miles round trip, totaling thirty-plus hours of driving time. I normally wouldn't go on a piano run of this distance for just one piano, but this was a piano owned by one special lady. Whether it was fate or goodwill, I was not going to disregard the wishes of the lady who loved her piano so much.

The next day, Michael called me after picking up the piano, with a problem he was having with the rental truck. None of the lights were working. He'd checked the fuses and that wasn't the problem, so it must be in the wiring harness. I suggested he stop and trade the truck for one that had working lights, but he didn't want to lose time on the road. He was going to take a chance and drive through the night with no lights; something I would never have done, but he was a bull.

I expected to get a call during the night from my son, or the police, about getting pulled over because of the non-working lights, but never did. Instead, I was pleasantly surprised when I arrived at work in Yonkers at 9 a.m. to see Michael and his helper waiting for me at the loading dock. He told me he drove all night with no lights and had no trouble because of it. I imagined that they had Loretta as their guardian angel to help them with a safe, trouble-free journey home.

A few years later, once again I received a call from Loretta's daughter, Corinne. This time she wanted to buy a piano. I couldn't have been happier to help her. This was my opportunity to give a piano back to her family. I found her a small Steinway upright for her home, which was just what she asked for.

By helping both women, mother and daughter, I knew I was doing exactly what I was meant to do as a career.

Even though life does not offer a crystal ball to see how your future might unfold, it's a good rule to be kind to people. Don't take advantage of a situation that might cause them pain or suffering, while you profit from their loss. I had no way of knowing if I'd ever see Loretta's Steinway again, yet . . .

Chapter 10

THE STEINWAY ON THE WALL

Traveling from state to state during the winter months in the northeast was difficult and dangerous. That's why a Steinway hunting trip to good old Florida was a midwinter's dream for me.

Heading south on I-95, knowing I would soon be feeling the warm Florida sun upon my face and that the piano moving would be easy, kept me cooking. Mostly no stairs, single-level homes, elevator buildings, and paved driveways. No snow, no ice, it was a piano mover's dream.

I received many calls from ads that I ran in most of the Florida newspapers. That made for a very busy Steinway buying venture, driving night and day through the Sunshine State.

Eleven days after my arrival in Florida, my truck was filled with some very old, and some not-so-old, Steinway grands. I would soon take them back to New York and offer them to the many rebuilders and retail dealers that I was supplying.

On my last day there, a call came from an elderly woman who told me of a Steinway grand piano she wanted to sell. She explained to me that she had owned it for many years and needed to sell it to raise money to care for her ailing mother. I was hoping that I would be able to help her out and land one last Steinway before heading north. I was on the east coast of Florida in the Palm Beach area when the call came in, and she was located in Daytona Beach. It was on the way home.

At that time there were no cell phones or GPSs, so the only communication between my seller and me was by pay phone. The seller would leave a message for me with a live answering service, and I would return their call to discuss the piano and get directions from them. Most of the time the person giving me directions really didn't know the roads too well outside of their local area, so finding my way to them was not always easy.

The nice lady gave me her address, and I headed north to Daytona. Once in the area, I opened my "Florida Map to Cities and Towns," and I looked up her street address. I drove to her area, and much to my surprise, found that she lived in a neighborhood with many run-down homes that needed a lot of work. I was sad to see how dilapidated this area was. I finally arrived at her little saltbox home, located in the middle of a housing development.

My helper and I went up to the front door and knocked. The door opened, and a short woman with long black hair and powder-white skin greeted us and invited us in. I was surprised at what I saw. As I walked through the house, I realized I was in a private nursing home. Wheelchairs and old-style hospital beds were everywhere. Every room was filled; the living room, dining room, and all of the bedrooms held elderly people in what seemed to me to be very poor health.

I was told by the woman who was offering me the Steinway that along with her mother, she was the caregiver for all of these people.

At least fifteen people were being cared for.

I looked around for a grand piano, but all I saw was a small brown spinet piano, up against the wall in the living room. At that point I'd felt as though I'd been tricked.

I asked her if that was the only piano in the house. She replied, "Yes." I felt bad for her, and bad for me. Time wasted for us both, as I had thought. Hers was an off-brand piano that I didn't have a need for or want. She begged me to buy it so she would have some money to feed the people she was caring for in her home.

I felt terrible about the whole thing. She offered me the piano for fifty dollars. It was then I noticed a hand-woven tapestry of a grand piano hanging on the wall above the spinet. The name Steinway & Sons was embroidered across the key cover. I asked her about this, and she replied, "I told you I had a Steinway!" We both smiled.

I offered to buy the tapestry for the same fifty dollars, and she said yes. I got the Steinway on the wall, she got the money she needed to feed her elderly residents, and she still had her piano.

It was the easiest piano move in my life, and I had to drive from New York to Florida to make it happen.

Chapter 11

ALMOST THE LAST TENNESSEE WALTZ

It was an extremely warm spring day in New York's picturesque Hudson Valley when I received a call from an elderly pastor who lived in the Smoky Mountains of Tennessee. His was a small town, but there was a big old stone church with an 1868 8'6" Style IV Steinway concert grand that he wanted to sell. This piano, in the day it was manufactured, was the most expensive and elegant grand piano in the entire Steinway fleet.

At the time this Steinway was manufactured, the grands were not lettered as they are now. (Today's letter system is S–5'1", M–5'7", O–5'10½", L–5'11", A1–6'2", A2–6'1", A3–6'4", B–6'10½", C–7'4", and D–8'11".) The letter series was started in 1878, just ten years after this concert grand was made. The Style series grands were also listed by size. They were Style I–6'8", Style II–7'2", Style III–8'6", and Style IV, also 8'6", but with a fully scalloped wood skirt around the entire bottom of the cabinet.

When I received the call from the pastor, he described the piano to me in great detail, including the story of how a local well-to-do woman had willed the piano to her parish. She wanted it to go to her church, where she thought it would look exquisite.

He told me that it had been owned by a woman who had played concerts in her home for her friends. She had played it up until just weeks before her passing at the age of ninety-seven. At that time, fifteen years prior to our conversation, the piano was presented to the church. She had loved her Steinway, and she loved to play it for her friends.

I asked him, "Why are you selling the piano now?"

He was silent for a moment, then replied, "It's not being played anymore, and I feel it should go to someone who would enjoy playing it, as the woman who once owned it would have preferred."

I thought that made sense, but I didn't have a helper available, so I asked him, "If I decided to buy the piano, could you provide me with a few people to help load the piano into my truck?"

He said that he would be able to arrange some helpers.

The next day I began my trip to the Smoky Mountains. It was a full day and night's travel.

This trip was another time when a cell phone and GPS would have been very helpful. But this was 1993, and I didn't own a cell phone yet. The pastor had asked me to call him once I was off the interstate, so I searched for a public phone.

I reached him at his home and explained where I was. The directions that he gave me from that point weren't easy to follow. There were few landmarks, and I was way up in the mountains. I did my best to follow his directions, but I got lost several times. I finally found the long, winding road that led to the small town where the church was located.

I stopped and used another public phone to call him. He asked me to stay where I was, and he would come to meet me. I waited for about five minutes, and he drove up in a beat-up old pickup truck. He got out of his truck and walked over to introduce himself to me. He was a frail man who looked to be in his late eighties. He explained to me in detail that I should not take any money out of my pocket in front of the helpers, or I might not get out of there alive.

I had already driven a long way. I was tired and hungry, and just wanted to load and return home to New York. However, I had a bad feeling now about going any further with this deal, thinking that I might possibly be risking my life. I took a deep breath and thought that if I did everything right, I could get this piano into the truck safely, and be on my way in a short time. I told the old pastor that it was his responsibility to make sure that I stayed safe during the loading process, and that I would give him the money to pay the helpers behind closed doors.

He agreed, and I followed him up a hill to another small town, then onto a narrow dirt road, through the woods to a cleared area where the church stood. This place was so far removed from anywhere that could be considered a town, that they would never have found my body if I had met my demise.

We each got out of our vehicles, walked up the stairs, and walked inside. The building was dark, damp, and dreary. The air was musty and heavy. There were a few small stained-glass windows that were held together with duct tape, and about fifteen chairs in the middle of the room. It was as though the church had been somewhat disassembled. There were no pews, nor was there an altar. But there was a small stage, and on it was a big Steinway grand waiting to be liberated from the hills of the Smoky Mountains. I walked over to it and inspected it to check its condition.

It was truly one of the rare ones; rosewood with large elephant-style legs, also known as Rococo style, with a fully scalloped wood skirt around the base of the cabinet and a delicately carved music rack. The good news was it was in all-original condition and never had been mistreated or abused, but it was certainly played hard for many years. It was a prime candidate for a complete restoration. I'm sure that in its heyday, the music that was played on this masterpiece Steinway rivaled any other brand of concert grand piano.

With the information and the serial number the pastor had provided to me previously, I had pre-sold it to a famous New York City restoration shop, contingent on my inspection. There, it would receive a state-of-the-art restoration.

The pastor and I dickered for a short time over the selling price, but finally we agreed, and we shook on it. He then led me into a small room behind the stage. He told me that it would be safe to count the money there. The room had only one window, which was facing my truck. I looked out the window to see three men peering into the windows of my truck. The hairs on the back of my neck stood up, and I was afraid that it might turn into a dangerous situation.

I told the pastor, "Before I take any money out of my pocket, you need to tell those men to get away from my truck."

He reassured me, "There is nothing to worry about as long as you don't offer them any money directly. Let me pay them once the piano is loaded into the truck. I don't think it's wise to let them see how much cash you have."

I needed to get out of this place as quickly as I could. I counted the money that I had agreed to pay him for the piano, plus the extra to pay the helpers. He stuffed the money into his front pocket and led me out to the front door.

We walked outside to my truck where the three beady-eyed, skinny, smelly, bearded mountain men, who looked like they hadn't had a bath in months, were waiting to help. I took my moving equipment out of the back of the truck: dolly, blankets, straps, and piano board. Luckily, I was able to back the truck right up to the church stairs, which were even with the truck ramp.

The pastor insisted on helping. It took all five of us to lift the Steinway off the floor and get the right front leg off, so that it could be lowered down onto the piano board. I blanketed it and strapped it onto the board. Then the pastor and his men helped me load it into the truck, where I strapped it securely to the right wall of the truck.

He walked them to the front of the truck and paid them for their work. Before they left, I thanked them and got into my truck. The pastor came up to my window and told me, "Do not stop to talk to anyone on the road. It could still be dangerous for you."

I locked my doors and drove slowly down the long, narrow dirt road. Once I reached the paved road on my way out of town, I hit the gas, never so glad to see the lights of civilization as I was then.

Chapter 12

OFF THE NOTCHES

It all started with a call that came in about a Steinway C grand piano, ebony color and Victorian style. Like the piano in the burned-down church, this piano dated from the 1880s.

At 7'4", this Steinway model C was the concert scale piano, sized just below the model D, which measured 8'11¾" and is the largest grand piano that Steinway has manufactured. If you were a serious pianist and didn't have the space to accommodate a D, you would choose a model C. This historic Steinway grand piano design is best known for being played by the legendary Steinway artist Ignacy Jan Paderewski during his famed concert tour of the United States in the early 1890s.

The reason that this piano was so unique is that the string-scale design brought five sets of double-wound bass strings into the tenor section, which made for a smoother transition of tone from the bass bridge to the tenor bridge. The model C was manufactured until 1911 but was available by special order until 1941. A smaller version of the same string-scale design was also used for the model A3, which was 6'4" in length, just one foot shorter than the model C. The model A3 was manufactured from 1913 to 1937. It was also available by special order until 1941. This was the "model C's little brother."

I contacted the Steinway factory with the serial number of the piano and found that it was first owned by Charles Goodyear Jr., of the Goodyear Tire & Rubber Co. It was a great find when you were not only going to buy a rare old Steinway grand, but when its provenance was connected to a well-known manufacturing family.

I contacted Mickey, a technician with whom I traded regularly, who lived in Michigan. He was always interested in special family Steinway pianos and thought that he'd be able to find a home for it if I decided to buy it.

This piano was in the tiny town of Pittsburg, New Hampshire, with a population of under 1,000, located at the very top of the state. From my home, this was 360 miles north. It was as far north as you could drive in New Hampshire before reaching Canada. It was in the dead of winter, with lots of snow, slippery driving, cold and icy conditions. With my truck pointed north and my trusted right-hand man, Jeffrey, at my side, we hit the trail. We started out around 7 a.m. to get a jump on traffic and the snowstorm that was forecast for that day. We were anticipating a long day of driving to the Steinway that had such a rich family history.

After driving over ten hours on what would have normally been a six- or seven-hour trip we finally reached Pittsburg. I needed better directions, so I stopped at a phone booth in the middle of the main street and got half blown over by a strong wind. Then we headed out for the last leg of our trip. We arrived at our destination, a large Tudor-style home on a big hill. It was a spooky-looking place, but at this point, nothing was coming between us and the front door.

A nice older gentleman who resembled the butler that you would see in an English movie invited us in. He told us that he was the best friend and housekeeper of the owner, who was currently in Europe. He was left in charge of caretaking the estate and selling the piano while the owner was away, as he was not going to return until spring. He showed us around the house, offering us interesting historical information about all the collectible artwork and furniture his good friend had accumulated in his long life.

He led us down a flight of stairs to a room, where we finally arrived at the Steinway. It was an all-original-condition Victorian model C with exquisitely carved fluted legs. The ebony varnish had a light patina. The piano looked magnificent in this setting, placed among the other rare antiques.

After inspecting the piano, we agreed on a price and started our loading process. I then looked around and realized that there was no way for the piano to be moved out of this room without going up one flight of stairs to the front door, where we had entered.

I asked the gentleman how they had moved the piano into this room when it was delivered. He replied that they'd come through one of the floor-to-ceiling windows to our left. He explained to us that the windows could be easily removed to enable large furniture to enter and exit this room without have to struggle with the stairs.

After hearing this good news, I asked the man if there was a driveway outside the windows. He said yes, and that the snow had been plowed there within the last two hours in anticipation of our arrival. We drove the truck around the house very carefully, so as not to slide off the driveway, for fear of getting stuck.

We backed up as close to one of the windows as we could, but there was a 6-foot-wide and 8-foot-deep drainage ravine between the house and the back of the truck, making it impossible for us to back up all the way. The truck had a 12-foot ramp that we had to extend all the way to get into the house. Still, it was a very tricky and dangerous move. Having the ramp extended all the way with no supports and no sides made me quite nervous, considering the weight of the piano, which was close to 1,000 pounds. The piano, the moving equipment, and two men totaled around 1,600 pounds. We decided it was a good idea to build supports with anything we could find on the property. We were allowed to go into a barn that contained wood and metal pieces, which we used to construct our supports. We packed up the piano in the house, removed the framework that held the window in place, put the ramp into the window jamb, and wheeled the piano into the truck.

Once it was secured in the truck, we went back into the house, where the butler had blackberry brandies waiting for us. We all toasted to our success in loading the piano, and to our safe trip home.

It was almost 10 p.m.; fifteen hours from when we'd started our trip. Now we faced the daunting realization that we still had a long trip back. The snow was coming down lightly, but steadily.

We were starving, but there were no open stores in sight. Once we got back on Route 3, we found a convenience store, gassed up, ate some junk food, and headed south.

About one and a half hours into our trip, we started our climb into the Franconia Notches. This is a well-known and dangerous strip of highway, with an elevation of 2,000 feet above sea level. It should only be traveled in nice weather, rather than on a cold, windy, snowy night.

It was now after 1:00 a.m. Jeffrey and I were both exhausted. The last thing we needed was to climb the most dangerous mountain in the Northeast, which was now covered in snow and ice, with the winds howling at us, and drive a big box truck over the bridge that connected the 2,000-foot drop into the Franconia Notches. Nevertheless, there we were, forging up the north side of the mountain with the heavy winds blowing the truck sideways. Suddenly, it slid into the left lane. I slowed to a complete stop, realizing that if I went any farther, the truck was going to blow over the side of the bridge. We were three feet away from the four-foot guard rail on the wrong side of the road. The wind was rocking the truck back and forth. I opened the driver's side door, jumped out of the truck, and told Jeff to abandon ship. He refused, saying he was staying in the truck.

I slammed my door and walked to the back of the truck, hoping and praying that the heavy winds would slow down. Suddenly, the wind stopped. I ran and jumped into the driver's seat, started the truck, and steered the wheel to the right. Slowly stepping on the gas, I drove forward off the bridge. I could not believe that just minutes before, I thought I was going to watch the truck and its contents – the Goodyear family's Victorian Steinway and my trusted right-hand man – blow over the side of the bridge.

Gasping in relief, we headed down the snowy road. We were tired and hungry, snow-blind and exhausted from this treacherous trip. We needed food and a few stiff nightcaps to bring this harrowing day to a close.

As we ventured on, we noticed a small sign, barely visible, that read "Mittersill Alpine Resort." We looked for a road or a driveway, but the snow was covering everything. There was a faint shadow of a road to the right, so we turned into it. After a few minutes of driving, the resort appeared like an angel in the night. However, it looked like it was closed, with only a few lights on. We pulled up in front, parked the truck, and walked to the door. We knocked, but no one answered. The door wasn't locked, so we opened it and entered a timeless and beautiful chalet, in an old-world Swiss design.

A few people were sitting inside at the bar, which we were told was about to close, so we ordered a few shots of scotch. After our drinks, we found a candy machine and bought as much junk as we could eat. It wasn't much of a dinner, considering the rough road we'd just traveled.

The front desk was closed, and we needed to get a room for the night. After looking around, we were confronted by a young man, who was the caretaker. We asked him if there were any available rooms. He said that there was one room left, so we took it. Lucky for us he was there, or we would have ended up sleeping on the floor.

Jeff and I went down to the basement, where we found an old, beat-up Ping-Pong table. We played and laughed until we couldn't stand up anymore, and finally decided to hit the beds.

We woke up to a bright sunny day. The snow had stopped falling, but the roads were completely covered. After a few hours, the snowplows went to work, and the driving was good enough for us to start our long journey home.

Once there, I called Mickey to let him know I'd purchased the piano. I gave him the details about its condition, and he was thrilled. We made a deal and arranged for the piano to be shipped to him, where he would find it a new home.

If the new owners only knew – but most likely never will – what an ordeal it was to retrieve this historic Steinway, they would probably treasure it that much more.

Chapter 13

WHEN THE ANGELS SANG TO THE CLYDESDALES

Every now and then I hear a sad story about a Steinway that was destroyed by a flood or fire. Whenever I'm told about one of these timeless treasures, I appreciate the chance to be involved in resurrecting one that has suffered this kind of horror.

In the middle of winter in the early 1990s, when I was traveling through Illinois, I was offered a Steinway model O; a 5'10" parlor grand, manufactured in 1914. This piano had barely survived a fire while sitting in one of the summer retreats of a very affluent and famous family whose products are sold worldwide and have been since 1876.

The call came to me about this piano from an antiques and collectibles dealer. The dealer had just been called in by an estate lawyer who was charged with cleaning out the remains of a house that was owned, and most recently occupied, by family members of the late August Anheuser Busch, Sr. A famous American brewing magnate, he was the president and CEO of Anheuser-Busch, based in St. Louis, Missouri, from 1913 to 1934. He is referred to as the father of Budweiser Beer.

The dealer had found my classified ad in a small local newspaper. He told me that the Steinway he had lying on the bed of his pickup truck had been destroyed in a fire and was not playable. Most of the case, keys, and all moving parts were charred from the flames, and the piano was soaked because it had crashed through the floor of the house and ended up in the basement, sitting in water for some time. He told me that the only part that was salvageable was the harp and the very badly burned and water-soaked rim of the piano, which held the harp in place. The lawyer told the antiques dealer that before the fire destroyed this Steinway, it had beautiful hand-carved ivory cupids all around the outside of the case. The dealer mentioned that you could still see the outlines of where they once were.

After a ten-minute conversation, I decided I wanted to meet with the man who was dragging around, in the back of his pickup truck, what he said had been the rare and beautiful Budweiser family Steinway. We set a time to meet the next day so that I could see this magnificent Steinway, with such a rich history, that had barely survived. He asked where I was traveling from and I told him that I was near Chicago. He said he would meet me at a rest stop on a highway outside of Springfield, Illinois.

I was very excited about the history of the piano, but not so sure it was a piano I wanted to get involved with. I intended to call Steinway customer service in Long Island City, New York, once I found a serial number on the piano. I wanted to find out if the serial number matched any records that could prove this piano was owned by August Anheuser Busch Sr., or any member of his family bearing the same last name. If so, this would prove to me that the antique dealer's tale was true. I set our meeting for 3:00 that afternoon so I would have plenty of time to call the Steinway factory to get the information, since they closed around 4:30 on weekdays.

I pulled in to our meeting place very close to 3:30. I didn't have much time to inspect the piano, find a serial number, and run a make with the Steinway factory to get the proof I needed to back up his story. There sat a beat-up old white pickup truck, open in the back, with nothing covering the piano from the elements. It wasn't snowing at that moment, but with the dark skies overhead and being that time of year, there was a good chance it could happen any time.

I got out of my car and walked over to the truck and introduced myself. I was truly amazed that this man had dragged a destroyed rim of a piano, with the harp still inside it, onto his truck, and was doing his best to find it a home and make a few bucks. My work has brought me to many places in my forty-plus-year career. I'm never too surprised at the Steinways I'm asked to look at with the idea that I would find them a new home. I have chosen this work, and I take it seriously.

This Steinway had no legs, no lid, no music rack, no pedals, and no key cover. The keys were burned and water-soaked beyond repair. The soundboard was burned so badly that it curled away from the rim inside the piano and was pointing up instead of lying flat in the piano. All the felt parts inside the hammer action had completely fallen off. All the laminated parts of the rim were separated and coming apart. The only thing that was salvageable was the harp, which had survived the fire. The most remarkable thing was that I could still make out the silhouettes of the ivory cupids. Their presence made this Steinway the heavenly art case that possibly had graced the home of the family known for the Budweiser Clydesdales. These small, but I'm sure, detailed ivory angels were placed on each side of the piano, as well as the front corners of the keyboard.

With little time to spare, I copied down the serial number from the harp of what I was hoping to discover was a very historic Steinway and called the customer service department at the Steinway factory. I was fortunate that, at so close to closing time, my friend Rose answered the phone. I gave her the serial number and told her that I was outside at a rest stop south of Chicago, staring at an old Steinway that I was considering buying. In her kind way, she let me know that it was just about time to close, but she would take a moment to get me the info.

After I waited on hold for a minute or so, she returned to the phone. She read the serial number aloud to make sure we were on the same page. I walked back and confirmed that this was the number, reading it right from the piano.

I listened closely, so as not to miss a word. Steinway's records showed that the piano was a model O grand, manufactured in 1914 and delivered to the Steinway dealer in St. Louis, Missouri, for owner August Busch. I thanked her for her time, told her that we would talk again soon, and wished her a good night.

So, there I was, with the sun setting quickly, standing with the dealer at the back of his truck in front of a Steinway that needed more restoration than I was willing to invest in. I believe, to this day, that the work to restore that piano would have been beyond any work that the Steinway restoration experts of our time had ever attempted. The dealer offered me the remains of that piano for fifty dollars, but I did not buy it.

I now look back on the opportunity that was offered to me:

having the chance to own the remains of a Steinway originally owned by that famous family. I still regret not having the vision that I could have possibly had it restored to its original glory, no matter what the cost would have been. It could have been proudly displayed in my home, as it was in their home, when the angels sang to the Clydesdales.

Chapter 14

62554

No matter when or where I planned my Steinway hunts, the advertising had to start running at least one month before the trip. I would get out the map, pick my farthest destination, and advertise in all the newspapers that had a "Wanted to Buy" classified section. The ad would read: "Steinway Grand Piano Wanted, any age in any condition. Will pay cash and pick up." Sometimes sellers would call within the first two weeks, but most of the calls would come in during the last two. After receiving many calls and talking for countless hours on the phone with Steinway owners about their pianos and their lives, I would have a list of possible sellers lined up.

This was the time to hit the road, while the sellers were waiting for me to come see and, they hoped, purchase their Steinways. I was excited to know that they were ready to invite me into their homes, having gained trust in me from our many telephone conversations.

My plan was to begin this trip at the end of the first week of August 1995. Sadly, I was not able to leave as planned. On the morning of August 6th, which would have been my late father's 79th birthday, my dear mother passed away. I had spoken to her on the phone the evening before, and we'd joked about having a small birthday cake for him to celebrate.

My mother, 78 years old, received her social security check on the 5th of each month. On the next day I would always take her shopping, and she would take me out to lunch. I would call her around 9 in the morning to arrange the time to pick her up. That morning I called, but she did not answer. I waited fifteen minutes and called again; still she did not answer. I waited a short time and tried her again, but no answer. In my heart, I didn't want to believe what I felt to be true.

I went out to my car and drove to her apartment, about fifteen minutes from my house. I put the key in the door and slowly opened it. I saw her resting with her eyes closed in her favorite recliner. I called to her, but she didn't answer. I walked over to her and put my face to hers. She was cold. I took a moment to gather my thoughts as I tried to make sense of what I knew had happened.

I dialed the operator and asked to be connected to the police department. I explained the situation, and they sent over an ambulance. After a few minutes they arrived. The paramedic confirmed that she had indeed passed. My carefully planned trip to the Midwest needed to be put on hold to make arrangements.

If you don't meet with the sellers and make the deal shortly after they have agreed to an appointment, often they lose interest in selling the piano to you. From experience, I'd learned that they may have told a few friends or neighbors their plan to sell it, or they might be consulting with another dealer to try to get a higher price. Family members might have an interest in buying it, or even have rights to it beyond the owner's right to sell it. I've even known people who have started to play their piano again and have had second thoughts about parting with it. In that event, I always suggest that they take all the time they need to decide before letting the Steinway leave their hands. I make it quite clear to them that my job is to bring music to people, not take it away.

After my mother's funeral arrangements were made, our heartbroken family put her to rest. Although I had taken little time to mourn her passing, I needed to take the trip that I had planned, since I had many Steinways lined up to buy. The only way to make this trip worthwhile was to keep as many appointments as possible, knowing that by now, some of the sellers might have lost interest.

I needed to start driving from my home around 5 p.m. My first stop was going to be just south of Chicago. If I timed it right, I would arrive there at noon the next day, just in time for lunch. Then I would rummage through a bunch of old barns, where the son of a gentleman farmer and piano technician known as "Ron the Piano Man" collected a great number of pianos. He would go to all of the piano dealers in Chicago several times each month and buy most of their used trade-ins. Every now and then I would get a good deal on a Steinway or two from him, so I always made a point of stopping in to see what he had. Over the many years of piano dealing, we had developed a friendship. Each time I visited Ron, he made sure that there were a few cold Budweisers in the fridge waiting. Along with his wife and partner in crime, Dorothy, we'd go out for a meal together.

Ron had a fun hobby: collecting Budman (the Anheuser-Busch mascot) paraphernalia. Whenever we talked on the phone, I referred to him as "Budman." Through my many miles of traveling, I would sometimes find a Budman collectible for him that he didn't have and would surprise him with it.

He had a nickname for me, too. While visiting with them over the years, I would tell them stories about my five children. They always enjoyed the stories because they'd never had children, and I felt as though they were experiencing the joys of parenthood vicariously. There was one story in particular that Ron got a chuckle out of. He asked me how I was greeted by my children when I returned from my road trips. I told him that rather than try to give them all a hug at the same time, I would lie on my back in the middle of the living room and let them all climb onto me at once, giving and getting as many hugs as we could. He laughed and replied, "Like an anthill." From that moment on, I was "Mr. Anthill."

With three hours of daylight left, I pulled out of my driveway and headed for the interstate highway that would take me west. I was still grieving the loss of my mother just five days before, but I needed to go.

Normally my piano-buying adventures were exciting; I didn't know much about who I would get the chance to meet, or the real truth about the history and condition of the next Steinway I was to encounter. Now, however, I wasn't excited to leave, knowing that when I returned, the woman who gave me life would no longer be there to greet me.

As I drove into the night, I remembered something my mother had told me a week after my father had passed away. I had a very hard time with the grieving process after he passed. I would sleep in his walk-in closet, where he hung all his suits, so I would feel close to him, and weep. She told me that in the Jewish religion it is believed that if I did not stop crying beyond the seven-day grieving period, he would not rest. So, I made myself stop. I had her in my life for twenty-one years after he passed. I took her advice and tried not to grieve too long for her, because I wanted her to rest in peace.

Sometime around 10 that night, I pulled into a rest stop near Buffalo. I called my voicemail to retrieve messages from my cell phone. There was one message, from a young man named Chuck, who was interested in selling a Steinway upright piano. At that time, I wasn't really interested in buying uprights, because most of the people who were buying from me wanted grand pianos. The one thing that intrigued me the most was that the phone number he left was from a Cleveland, Ohio, area code.

Cleveland was the one city that I rarely received calls from. Even after many years of advertising regularly in all the local *Pennysavers*, weekly papers, and dailies, I could never seem to break through. The reason was that there were two brothers, very well-known in the used Steinway trade, who ruled the town when it came to knowing when used Steinways went up for sale. On the rare occasion that I did get a call, it was always a struggle to see the piano before they would swoop in and beat me to the punch. The only time it seemed that I would have a chance to get into a Steinway seller's home before them was if the call came in and the timing was right. I would need to be passing through Cleveland on my way from New York to Chicago, or on my return trip.

By coincidence, if I continued driving as I planned to, I would be in Cleveland by midnight. I was sure no one would want to meet with me at that late hour, but I called him and told him that I was about three hours from Cleveland, and would be passing through that night on my way to Chicago. I also let him know that I would not be returning to New York on the same route, so if he wanted to sell his piano, tonight would be the night. He said that he would like to sell it if I could stop on my way to Chicago. He gave me directions, and we set an approximate time that I would arrive.

Once I reached Cleveland, the drive to his home was tricky. I had to travel down a very steep hill, through a dark and dreary industrial area. It appeared that I was going into an area that I didn't belong in at that late hour, or possibly not going to a respectable person's home. I almost turned around and drove away.

I pulled over to the side of the narrow road, which ran along a very large body of water, and gave Chuck a call. I let him know that I did not feel safe driving through the area, and I was going to turn around and leave. He asked me what landmarks there were that I could describe to see if I was anywhere near his house. I gave him a few, and he told me I was getting very close. At that moment, I needed to make a decision whether or not to continue to follow his directions or drive away.

Nervous and confused, but still excited about what I was hoping would break the streak of no-buys in Cleveland, I continued. Chuck stayed on the phone with me as I drove along the Cuyahoga River until I arrived at his driveway.

I turned onto the dark roadway and drove for a short time, until it opened up to a breathtaking view of Cleveland and his castle-like Italianate mansion. A magnificent sight, it proudly sat on the water's edge with large white marble statues gracing the front of the home, and smaller ones surrounding the circular driveway. I was awed by the setting, and the fact that he was allowing me to come into his home at nearly 2 a.m. As I pulled up closer to the front door, Chuck turned on the spotlights in front of the house and came out to greet me. A young man who looked to be in his late twenties, he explained why he did not mind my coming to see the piano at this unlikely hour.

The house had belonged to his father, who had passed away a

few months before. The house and all its contents were left to him, and he had recently decided to sell the house and needed to liquidate all of the furniture, including the piano.

After a few minutes, Chuck invited me into his home. Looking around the magnificent foyer, I was stunned at the volume of marble statues and elaborate gold picture frames holding Renaissance oil paintings. He asked me to follow him down a dimly lit spiral staircase that led to what I thought was going to be the basement. Once we were at the bottom of the staircase, he turned up the lights in the room, and I was amazed at what I saw.

I was standing in the middle of a casino. The room was circular and was surrounded with huge floor-to-ceiling windows that offered a breathtaking view of the city as it sat nestled along the river's edge. This room was large enough to seat at least eighty people. To my right were a half dozen blackjack tables; to my left, a few craps tables. In front of me were a few roulette tables surrounded by slot machines. Behind those was a very large, fully stocked bar. The bar took up most of the wall on the far side of the room, and the casino took up the entire bottom floor of this huge house.

I asked Chuck if the piano was down here. He replied yes and pointed to the far left corner of the room, where it was covered by a tarp. He walked me over to unveil the first Steinway piano that was offered to me for sale in Cleveland. Even if I had no use for this piano, I would have to buy it just to break the spell. Chuck lifted the tarp off of the piano. At first glance, this piano did nothing for me, especially at that hour of the morning.

I shook off my weary attitude and took another look. It became more interesting at second glance. The piano was neck-high, about 45 inches or so, and was a dark reddish-brown color. The most distinctive feature was the front legs, which bowed in toward the bottom of the piano from underneath the keyboard, a Duncan Phyfe design. This was not a leg that I'd seen before on a Steinway upright, but I knew the style because I had studied the history of famous furniture designers that Steinway had commissioned. The two front panels that covered the hammer action were also unique, delicately carved with intricate detail. I became convinced that this was a great find.

Steinway was known for commissioning famous furniture designers, such as Thomas Chippendale, who was famous for the ball and claw design; Herter Brothers of New York who, among other things, made the furniture for the Red Room of the White House during the administration of Ulysses S. Grant; and Walter Dorwin Teague, who was known best for his mid-century modernism designs.

Prior to looking inside to inspect the mechanical condition, I asked Chuck if he had a price in mind. He replied that he did and told me what he was asking. Since the piano appeared to be from the 1870s to 1880s, his price seemed reasonable.

The next step was to open the top of the piano, remove the front panel, and find the serial number. I was very tired at this point and needed to be careful when removing the front panel, so as not to damage it. Now, with the top folded back and the front panel off of the piano, the serial number was visible. It was stamped into a wood laminate veneer that protected the pin block, off to the left front, above the treble tuning pins. The number was 45526.

I took a moment to read it again because it seemed like a series of numbers that were familiar to me, but I couldn't figure out why. Then it hit me; the serial number was my birthdate, backward; June 25, 1954. I froze for a moment and stared at the number. I had to believe that it was more than just the piano I was led to that night. Perhaps I was called there to meet a piano that held my birth numbers. The piano peered at me from the inside, as I looked at it from the outside.

After a few moments of silence, Chuck asked me if I was interested. I got a grip on myself and looked away from the serial number so I could focus on the mechanical condition of the piano. It was in all-original condition, and very well preserved. I told him that the tuner-tech who'd serviced the piano for his father had done a good job. The piano was right up to pitch, and I could feel that it was well regulated. When a piano is regulated properly, all the keys will be level and play evenly.

With this purchase, I would not only be breaking my dry spell, but I would be leaving with the piano that bore the numbers of my birthdate. I had also become acquainted with a young man who had recently lost his father, as I had just lost my mother.

I extended my hand, and we shook on the price. We were both relieved; Chuck knowing it was one less thing in his home that he had to deal with, and me for all the reasons that were important about purchasing this Steinway. He helped me bring my moving blankets, straps, and dolly into the casino through a back door. After I paid him, he kindly assisted me in loading the piano into my truck. Once the piano was secure, Chuck and I said a friendly good-bye.

It was just past 3 a.m., and I was exhausted. I drove out of his driveway and backtracked through the dark streets of the industrial area that I'd traveled through an hour or so before.

Once I was back on the interstate, heading toward Chicago, I pulled into a rest stop to gather my thoughts. It had been over twenty hours since I woke the day before, and I knew it was best to take a break.

My original plan was to drive straight through to Chicago and have breakfast with "Budman" and his wife that same day, but this couldn't happen unless I continued with no sleep. I looked at my road map to figure out how long it would take to get to them. I had another five hours of driving if I was going to meet that goal. I decided to stop and take a rest.

I moved my 18-foot box truck into the trucker's rest area, which was the safest place to sleep at that hour. I took out a blanket and pillow, kicked back the seat, and drifted off into a deep, long-overdue sleep.

When the sun rose at seven, I did too. I took a stroll into the truck stop, washed up, ate a quick breakfast, and got back on the highway. I called Budman to let him know I would be getting to his shop at about noon, and we firmed up a lunch date. As I pulled into his driveway, he came out to greet me with a big smile. I quickly got out to greet him. "Mr. Anthill," he called out. "Budman," I shouted back. We told a few jokes and headed to the restaurant. His wife was busy that day, so it was just us piano men.

After lunch, we went back to his barns, where he tried to convince me to buy every piano he owned. Why not? I was a piano addict, and he was a piano pusher. But Budman knew I only wanted Steinways. He only had a few, which I bought.

Normally, I would never have a beer in the middle of the day with many miles ahead of me to drive, but I couldn't turn down one from Budman. We each had a cold one and shared a few more laughs. As he walked me out to my truck, I noticed a freshly poured concrete sidewalk beside his garage—an invitation for us both to write our nicknames. So we did, and with a heartfelt handshake, said good-bye.

Out to the highway I went once more. I needed to try to keep eight more appointments with potential sellers in Illinois, Michigan, Indiana, Ohio, and New York. Along the many miles of travel, I took time to reminisce and mourn the loss of my mother.

After seven days on the road, I had purchased eleven pianos. I didn't get them all, but I was very satisfied with the ones I did.

As the sun was setting on the seventh day, I found myself outside of Binghamton, New York. I was only three and a half hours from home, so I kept driving. Once I arrived, I found my whole family asleep, so I missed my normal anthill greeting.

After a short time, all the Steinway grands I'd purchased on this trip got sold to, and picked up by "Steinway Dan Wilson" of Atlanta, Georgia. The only piano that remained was the upright that I had bought in Cleveland. With all the facts that made this piano special to me, I decided to move it into the living room of my house. In the short time it was there, I took many photographs and researched its history with the Steinway factory.

I really wanted to keep it, but I knew it had great value to someone who would want a fine piece of Steinway history, along with the magnificent cabinet design. If it was meant for me to meet this piano that held my birth numbers stamped on the inside, then I should find it the home it deserved. I advertised it for sale, along with a comprehensive description of the condition and the rarity of the cabinet. If it sold, I would know that I had done my job. If it didn't sell, then it was mine to keep. One thing was for sure: I was going to put a very high price on it. If someone wanted it, they were going to pay well for it.

In the week that followed, I ran an ad in *The Yorktown Pennysaver*, a shopping guide in which my ads had successfully sold many pianos previously. Toward the end of the second week, I received a call from a woman who was very interested in seeing the piano. She said it sounded exactly like the style of Steinway upright she had been looking for. It was almost as though she knew the piano before she saw it. Apparently, she was a fan of Steinway, Duncan Phyfe furniture, or both. We made an appointment for the next day, and she arrived with her husband around 10 a.m.

I greeted them at the door and they entered the living room. The moment she laid eyes on the piano, her face lit up with a big smile. Her husband also took to it quickly. I knew I was going to lose that piano and make them the next happy owners.

They told me that they had recently purchased an old church. They were in the process of renovating the building to live in and to use as their offices. They went on to say that the furniture of the piano, especially the cutout gingerbread carvings in the two front panels, matched the decor in the main chapel almost perfectly. I was ready to offer them a little break on the price, just to move it along, when she asked how soon I could have it delivered. I said I could deliver it on that same day.

Not only did they agree to take delivery that day; I said I would follow them home with it. I told them I needed a little time to call up a helper with a small truck, and would be ready to roll in an hour. I offered them a few suggestions about places where they could get lunch while I was getting the piano ready to move. On their way out to eat, they could not stop thanking me for selling it to them. I told them that I was very happy that they were the ones getting it, because this piano was very special to me. I never did tell them all the reasons why.

After my helper, Jeff, and I loaded the piano into the truck and secured it for the short trip to the town in which they lived, the couple returned, and I followed them home. Once we arrived, I was feeling sad with the thought of letting the piano go.

I slowly opened the back of the truck, knowing I might never see the piano again. It was almost as if I was letting a part of myself go. Nevertheless, it was time to deliver. We pulled the ramp out from underneath the truck, I hopped up in the back, and untied and unveiled my piano. It was still mine, because they hadn't yet paid me for it. After taking it off the truck, we rolled it through the front door of the converted church into the chapel. We made our way to the front of the room, where we were asked to place the piano.

The lady could not have been more correct. The cutout carved panels in the front of the piano matched almost identically the wood design on the walls. I knew immediately that the piano belonged here. Most of the anxiety I'd felt up to that point dissipated. In all its glory, the Steinway I had called my own was now in the good hands of the two people who would care for it next.

To this day, I feel that my mother was the reason I came into that piano. With those serial numbers, I was sure it was her way of giving me faith in myself to endure her passing, and to let me know that even though I didn't take the traditional time to mourn for her, I was given a blessing. I took it as a sign that she was okay with me making that trip.

The money that I earned from this piano was used as part of the down payment to purchase a home that my large family moved into shortly thereafter. It was a home my mother never got to visit while she was alive, but I feel that it was one she helped me buy.

Chapter 15

O MY SHOULDER

One hot summer day in the mid-1990s, I received a call from a retired piano teacher, Gloria, from New Hampshire. She was responding to an ad that I had placed in her local newspaper.

She told me that the arthritis in both of her hands was making it impossible for her to play her 1909 Steinway parlor grand, 5'10" model O. Sadly, she felt it was time to part with it. She was hoping that I could find it a new home with someone who would enjoy playing it, as she had. This is a wish that I've heard so many times in the past. It breaks my heart to hear that someone who loves to play the piano can no longer continue playing.

She described her Steinway as being in all-original condition. It had an ebony case with ivory keys that had no chips or cracks. Her piano tuner had recently tuned it, and told her that it was holding its tune very well. It sounded like a piano that I wanted to buy.

I asked Gloria, "What would be involved in moving the piano from your house into my truck if I decided to buy it?"

She replied, "It's located on the first floor, and there's only one step out of the house."

The move sounded very easy. I felt that I could handle the move on my own, so I decided to travel solo.

The following day I started from my home around noon. With map in hand, I had all the information that I needed to find her house. I was looking forward to the scenic drive to the beautiful state of New Hampshire.

After what turned out to be a long and tedious six-hour drive, I pulled into Gloria's driveway as the setting sun painted a brilliant kaleidoscope of colors across the sky. Her home was a darling little white New England cape.

I walked up to her front door. I needed to visit with her, see the piano, and make a quick decision whether to buy it or not. If I did, I would have to break it down, load it into the truck myself, and have a long drive home that night.

Before I had a chance to knock, the door opened. I was greeted by a short gray-haired lady with a grand smile.

I introduced myself, and Gloria escorted me into her home. I noticed all of the miniature busts of famous classical piano composers she had on display. It was obvious to me, after looking around her home, that piano music was a huge part of her life. I realized then that her comfort was much more important than my profiting from her piano.

The one thing I try to make clear to a person who has finally made the difficult decision to part with their beloved piano is that I'm not there to take their music from them. If they feel, in any way, that I'm doing that if they sell their piano to me, I can't buy it. I make certain that they're ready to part with their piano. I assure them that I will find it a new home, with a pianist who will love it as they had. When I explained this to Gloria, she assured me that she was ready to part with her instrument. I was relieved that she was comfortable with her decision.

She showed me to the piano, which was in a small bedroom off her tiny kitchen that she used as her teaching studio. Moving it out of this small room was going to be much harder than I had anticipated. I expected it to be in a living room or parlor, where pianos were usually located.

The piano had never been restored and was in surprisingly fine condition for a 90-year-old Steinway. After a little haggling on her high asking price, I gave in and paid a bit more than I normally would have.

Now I had the daunting task of trying to figure out how to break down this 5'10" by 5' grand piano that was sitting in a 7' by 6' room without killing myself. There was barely enough space to take the legs off and place the piano on a dolly. If I'd had a second person to help me, it would have been a lot easier. There was no way Gloria could help me, and it was now long after dark. The house was far from any of the local bars, where I could have hired a few helpers. I was in it all alone.

Gloria let me know that she was frightened for me to do this by myself. I put her at ease, explaining to her that I had moved many pianos that size before by myself, although never from a space this small.

I went out to the truck and brought in my tools, dolly, screwdriver, straps, ropes, and blankets. I couldn't bring in a piano skid, which is a flat, padded board that the piano normally is laid down on to transport. It wouldn't fit into the room, under the piano, and still give me enough room to get the piano out. The only way that I was going to get that piano out of the room was to take off the lid and lay the piano on the dolly as I took the legs off.

With the music desk and rack out of the piano, and the lid taken off, I placed the dolly next to the long side of the piano, almost against the wall. I came around to the left front side of the piano, lifted it up, knocked off the left front leg, and lowered the corner of the piano down onto the dolly.

Then I had to get the piano up off the other two legs by lifting it in an upright position on the dolly, which was a trick. I had very little room to get on the right side of the piano since it was still almost up against the wall. I managed to get under the right side and lift it up with my shoulder until it was flat on the dolly, or so I thought.

Once I was in an upright position with the piano standing almost straight up on the dolly, I let it stand on its own just for a split second, and it started to fall back on me. I had nowhere to go but under the bottom of the piano, as it was falling on me. Six hundred and eighty pounds of Steinway O was riding down my right shoulder. I struggled to hold the piano up, and not let it fall too fast, so that it wouldn't collapse on me. I was fortunate that one of the wooden beams under the center of the piano was where my shoulder was, and was acting as a runner, sliding against me as I broke the piano's fall. I was pinned flat on the floor.

The noise it made when it came down on me was loud. Gloria came running into the room, screaming, "Are you okay?" I said yes, but she didn't believe me. She insisted on calling the police or an ambulance. I calmly but firmly reassured her that I was okay; I just needed a moment to get the piano off me. She was still insisting that she wanted to call in some help, and at that moment I knew I needed to act fast.

I gathered up all the strength that I had, got into an almost elephant-like position under the piano, and lifted it off me. Up, up, and back onto the dolly, where I held it just long enough to pull it away from the wall. Once it was standing upright on the dolly, I went around the piano to find out what caused it to fall back on me. To my surprise, there was a lamp plugged into an outlet in the wall. The plug was sticking out just enough to have stopped the piano from standing up straight, so when I pushed it up against the wall the first time, while it was standing on the dolly, it caused the piano to lean back on me and fall over. Now that the piano was standing upright on the dolly, with no chance of tipping over, I pulled the plug from the wall. Then I pushed the piano up against the wall to keep it secure. Gloria and I appraised the damage to my right shoulder.

She finally calmed down, realizing that I didn't get crushed by her piano. I realized that I had some mending to do on my right shoulder.

She brought me into her bathroom, where we proceeded to address my wound. My brown T-shirt was embedded into my skin where the 680-pound piano had ridden me to the floor. The three-inch by one-inch blood stain on my shirt needed to be pulled away from the open wound, and I wasn't letting anyone touch it but me. As I pulled it away from my shoulder, blood gushed out. Gloria kept a clean towel pressed against it for twenty minutes until the bleeding slowed. It wasn't a deep wound; it was a tear of the skin. It was very painful and left a visible scar that still reminds me of that day when a solo piano move went terribly wrong.

Once I was cleaned up, she gave me a man's button-down shirt to wear and I went back to continue moving the piano.

I strapped the piano to the dolly, securing it, and wheeled it to her front door. She stood next to it and steadied it as I backed the truck up to load it. I positioned the ramp and pushed the piano into the truck. After tying it down securely, I went back into her house.

We were both exhausted from our "friendly visit." I knew I had a long trip ahead of me, so I thanked her for her help and we said our good-byes.

As I pulled out of her driveway, and looked back at her house, I knew that I had done the best that I could to help her. The piano that she loved was on its way to find a new home and I felt good about that, even if I had some recuperating to do.

The T-shirt that I wore that day was a badge of honor for me. I held on to it for many years.

Chapter 16

TALL, DARK, AND HANDY

My mother was born and raised in Utica, New York, along with her three sisters and two brothers. My father was born and raised in Newburgh, New York, and he had two sisters.

In 1939, when my father was twenty-three, his uncle offered him a position managing a wholesale carpet and linoleum warehouse in Utica. My father decided to accept the job, and moved into the YMCA while he looked for an apartment. During his stay at the Y, he became friends with my mother's oldest brother, Bill. Since my father's family was approximately 180 miles away, Bill invited him to his parents' house for dinner. That was where he was introduced to my mother. It was love at first sight.

My grandparents had an older upright piano. My father sat down and started to play "Rhapsody in Blue," composed by George Gershwin in 1924. It was my mother's favorite piece, and he stole her heart.

After my mother passed, I found two vinyl 78 rpm recordings of "Rhapsody in Blue." One was his, and one was hers. It's as if they were meant to be together from the moment he played that song for her. They were married, and she gave birth to their first and only daughter soon after.

Since my mother was from Utica, I was no stranger to the city. We visited my aunts, uncles, and cousins often for important family events. In the summers, while in my early teens, I took the train by myself from Poughkeepsie to Utica to stay with my favorite aunt and uncle: Dorothy, my mother's sister, and her husband, Morris.

After my father's sudden passing in 1974, a lot of things changed drastically. Most of the traveling to Utica stopped, except to visit an occasional ailing relative. Soon after that, I was raising a family of my own and rarely visited.

In late fall of 1995, I had advertising running full-time all over the United States, with calls coming in daily from Steinway owners wanting to sell. One of the papers that I advertised in was *The Utica Observer-Dispatch*, Utica's daily newspaper. In 2017, it celebrated its 200th birthday, which would have been my mother's 100th birthday.

One call came in from that paper. It was from a man in charge of selling two older Steinways that were in the Masonic Lodge and weren't being used anymore. I made an appointment to inspect the pianos a few days later. It would be the first stop on my next trip. This time I was hoping to add to the family history in Utica by procuring Steinways there.

As I was ready to leave, I needed to turn my rented 15-foot yellow Ryder box truck around in my driveway but could not because I was boxed in by my car. I always left one set of keys to my car sitting on its front seat, so I knew where they were. I opened the driver's door, and to my surprise, the keys weren't there. I went into the house to look for them but had no luck. I had a second set stashed away in a safe place, so I moved the car, turned the truck around, and headed out of the driveway. I didn't give much thought to the missing keys, knowing that they would turn up when I returned from my trip.

As I reached Utica and found the Masonic Lodge, the sun was starting to set. I parked my truck in front of the building, went to the front door, and knocked. An older gentleman opened the door and invited me in. We had spoken on the phone a few hours before, so he was expecting me.

The lighting was very dim, which made getting a good look at the pianos very difficult. The ceilings were extremely high, and the few bulbs were not supplying any direct light. He handed me a box of old flashlights, but none of them were functional. After switching batteries and bulbs around, I finally assembled a flashlight that worked.

The first piano he showed me was a 1953 Steinway model D concert grand. It had the 100-year anniversary emblem affixed to the right side of the key cover, and also displayed the busts of the first Steinway makers. This was a rare find that had never been restored but was still in good original condition. To this day, it is the only 1953 D I have ever seen.

The second piano was an old Steinway Victorian upright piano. It was very tall, and ebony in color. I compared the serial number with my chart. It was from 1887, in all-original condition. It looked good and played well. Both Steinways had been well cared for over the years, and I wanted to buy them. I made my best offer, and we agreed on the price.

I asked him if he knew the history of the two pianos; who might have previously owned them, and how long they had been in the Masonic building. He told me that the large Steinway grand had been donated by a family whose father was a long-standing member of that Masonic Lodge. It was bequeathed to the Lodge upon his death, approximately twenty years before. The upright was already there when he became a member in 1935.

Immediately I flashed back twenty years, remembering that my mother gave me my father's jewelry case when he passed away. In that box was his Mason's pin. When I asked her why he had it, she told me that when they first met, he was a member of the Masonic Lodge in Utica. If the tall, dark Steinway upright I just purchased was in that Masonic Lodge since before 1935, then my father undoubtedly played it. I was amazed that I had found a Steinway that my father most certainly entertained on 56 years prior. It was one of the most poignant moments that I'd ever experienced. I didn't share this information with the caretaker; it was too personal.

The next step was to get both pianos loaded into my truck. Since I was traveling solo, I needed to hire a few strong arms. I asked him where the nearest local bar was, and he told me that it was on the next corner on the left. I told him I'd be back with the helpers. He smiled, and I took a walk to the corner bar. I offered a few bucks to a couple of strong-looking guys to help me with the move. We got them loaded quickly.

Once the pianos were safely in the truck, I paid my helpers and they headed back to the bar. I thanked the man for all of the information, as well as staying so late to sell me the pianos. He thanked me, too.

I sat in the truck for a few minutes staring at the building, wondering what it must have been like to be inside when my father was playing the piano. I drove away with that wonderful thought.

As I headed west on Interstate 90 on my way to more Steinway buys, I wondered who I was going to offer this Steinway piano to;

the piano that had had the same music played on it that I'd heard played many times at home, years later, by my father. If I was going to sell it to anyone, it needed to be someone who would appreciate it as much as I did, but for their own reasons.

After a long week of driving and piano buying, I returned home. My truck held eight Steinway grands and one Steinway upright. The grands were already pre-sold, and I delivered them within a few days. I sold the concert grand from the Masonic Lodge to a rebuilder and good friend in Indiana a few days after I purchased it. I struggled with selling the upright, knowing I wasn't going to keep it, even though it held a special place in my heart. I knew there was someone on my path waiting for this piano, and I hoped to meet them soon.

After a week, the piano was still sitting in the truck outside my house, and I was beginning to feel bad. I wanted it to go into the hands of a person who always wanted a piano just like this. A 108-year-old Victorian Steinway upright piano, in very well preserved, original condition like this one did not come along often. I didn't want to sell it to a dealer, but rather offer it to someone that I knew, a friend, relative, or possibly a close business associate. This way I'd know who would have it, and I'd be the one to service it and keep it tuned.

In the week that followed, I offered it to a few friends and told them I would sell it to them for the same price I paid. The piano was worth five times that in monetary value and held priceless historic value to me, but all they wanted were grands.

Two years earlier, I'd worked with a local real estate agent, an old family friend, who listed a house for rent that I was interested in. My family was growing fast, and we'd outgrown the house we were living in.

I had her ask the owners if they would be interested in renting with option to buy. They told her they were planning to sell the house but wanted to wait for at least two years for the housing market to improve. They decided to take me up on my offer. I would rent the house for two years with the understanding that they would hold one-fourth of the rent, in addition to a down payment toward the purchase price. The purchase price would be determined at the conclusion of the rental agreement, based on current market value. We moved in soon after.

It was nearing the end of our rental agreement, and it was time to make an offer on the house. I called my real estate agent and made her an offer that I'm sure she never expected. She knew of my piano work. From time to time, she mentioned that she'd love to have a Steinway in her home. The owners of the house had originally listed it for $189,000. I had a very specific budget of $150,000. My first offer had been for $145,000. They countered with $172,900, which didn't work for me. However, I now had a new player in the game: it was tall, dark, and it had Steinway written on it.

I told her that I had a Victorian Steinway upright piano in the truck outside of my house that I was sure would look marvelous in her home. She told me that she'd be right over to see it. A few minutes later, she sped into my driveway. I opened the overhead door, got into the truck, and took off the straps and blankets to unveil the piano. She climbed in the back of the truck and with a big smile asked, "So, how much do I have to pay for this?" I said, "Not one cent, but I have a plan, if you're willing to play along." She replied, "I'm listening."

I told her that my final offer on the house was $151,000. My real budget was $150,000, but since the number in my offer was the proof of my favorite rum drink, we could hold the price right there. I told her if she'd help facilitate the purchase of the house at $151K, I would move the Steinway into her house as a gift, the day after we closed on the sale. We went back to her office, drew up the new offer, and submitted it. A few days later, my offer was accepted.

When I returned home, I realized that I had been in such a hurry to get over to her office and make the offer on the house that I'd never blanketed and tied the piano back into the truck, so I went out to do that. As I was climbing out of the back of the truck, I looked down at the gravel driveway, and noticed something very shiny. I walked over to it and kicked the stones away, revealing the set of keys that weren't on the seat of my car the day I left, two weeks before. I bent down to pick up the keys and looked to my right. Joel, my four-year-old son, was standing beside me with a terrified look. Before I could say a word, he said, "Oh Daddy, I'm so sorry." I asked him, "Why are you sorry?" He replied, "I hid your keys under the stones, so you couldn't leave." He added, "When you leave in your truck, it makes me sad because you're gone too long."

I felt awful for him, but at the same time I had to give him credit for his crafty move. I chuckled at what he had done, picked him up, and gave him a big hug. I told him I would try to not leave for so long anymore. He smiled at me and asked, "Are you mad at me for hiding your keys?" I told him I wasn't angry at all. Apparently when he hid the keys, he thought that they were for the truck.

Since the piano had been sitting in the truck for over two weeks. and my house deal was in place with a closing date set, I moved the Steinway into my real estate agent's home. We were both more than satisfied with the way things worked out. I was about to purchase this large home, where my family could continue to grow and enjoy a comfortable lifestyle, and the Steinway that was so dear to me had found a new home with someone who adored it.

Chapter 17

THE LIBRARY B

A young woman in her early twenties visited Eastman School of Music in Rochester, New York, one summer. She was from Maine, where she had been attending school. She had planned to return to school at the end of that summer to finish her final year, but never did. Instead, what was to be a short visit to Eastman as an intern turned into a career as the school librarian that lasted until her retirement, some forty years later.

The stories that come about by bringing treasured Steinways back to the music marketplace are one of the most satisfying aspects of my work. They make the long road to my eventual success worthwhile. This is the story of a young woman's dedication to music schooling, and the Steinway that was by her side throughout her career.

She called me about ten years after she retired. She had kept her favorite piano by her side, until she made the decision to downsize her home. We agreed that I would go to Rochester to see it.

As I pulled out of my driveway, the snow was falling steadily. The trip was cold and icy.

When I got there, she offered me a cup of tea and relayed the story of her career and how her Steinway was always part of it. She told me that she had never married and had no children. Her career and her piano were the most important parts of her life. When she finally decided to retire as a school librarian, a precious gift was given to this sweet woman: her longtime companion, the 1916 Steinway 6'10" grand piano model B that had been in the library since it was new.

I inspected the piano and found that it was in all-original condition and had never been restored. It had several cracks in the soundboard, the hammers were worn, some of the ivories were chipped, and the cabinet had loose and missing veneer. It was a candidate for a complete restoration, yet it played well and sounded magnificent.

I wanted to buy her piano so I could make sure it would go to someone who would love it and care for it, as she had, for all those years.

After we agreed on a price, I had to figure out how to load the piano into the truck by myself. Her house was tiny, and there wasn't much room to maneuver the piano out of the front door. As I backed the truck up to the door, she guided me so that the ramp would go into her living room. I got in and out of the truck several times, as she was frail and couldn't handle the ramp. Once the ramp was in position, I brought in my moving equipment and packed the piano. I lifted it up on one side and she helped me by positioning the dolly beneath it. As she did, a veil of sadness fell over her face.

I asked her if she would be able to assist me in guiding the piano onto the ramp. As sad as she was to see it leave, she took a deep breath and agreed to help. Once the piano was in the truck and secured, I thanked her and reassured her that I would do my best to find a suitable home for her longtime companion.

The story of the music librarian from Rochester is forever in my heart.

Chapter 18

MONKEY BID

I am usually adventurous, but I'm cautious as often as I feel the need. After this purchase, I always looked for signs of deceit when dealing with private sellers.

You never get the truth about the seller's real reason for parting with their precious Steinway until you are one-on-one, face-to-face, standing next to their piano. Not until I met with this elegant ninety-three-year-old Southern belle, who had all intentions of running me around like a monkey on a string, had I ever been tricked so well.

Daisy, the wealthy widow of a prominent local doctor, called me from an ad that I had placed in a Greenville, South Carolina, newspaper. She offered to sell me her late husband's piano. It was a 1926 9-foot Steinway concert grand. She was an absolute joy to chat with on the phone about her love for her late husband and the lavish lifestyle that she had lived. She told me that her parlor, the place where the Steinway stood, was where her friends and family gathered. They came to sing, dance, and listen to the great pianists her husband would hire to bring music into their home. But now, after his passing and with all those great memories, it was time for the piano to be sold.

Keys in hand, and gas tank full, I headed out to the land of cotton. Luckily for me, it was a sunny day in the middle of summer, so the driving was easy. No snow, no ice; just open-window fresh-air driving.

On this trip I partnered up with a friend who lived near me, Michael John, who also had a great passion for Steinways and was involved in many of his own piano restoration projects. He was interested in the long-distance piano-buying process and also enjoyed the long drives that led to the Steinways we were hunting. The distance from my house to her home in South Carolina was 803 miles; driving time twelve hours.

Normally, I would not have taken such a long drive for only one piano, but after the many intriguing conversations I had with Daisy about her life and her husband's Steinway, I thought it would be a worthwhile trip.

We started our long journey at 6 a.m. on a weekday, so that we would arrive around dinner time. The plan was to visit with her during the early evening, find out about the history of the piano as she knew it, inspect the piano to make sure it was a Steinway I wanted to buy, and pay her the agreed-upon price. If all went as planned, we would load the piano into the truck, get a good night's rest at a local motel, and be back on the road early the next day, heading home to New York.

Much to my surprise, what was to be a simple meeting with a woman who seemed to be a very sweet and honest Southern belle, turned into a two-day buying circus.

We pulled up in front of her very large one-story home. I rang the doorbell, and a lovely middle-aged woman, Daisy's housekeeper, answered the door. She escorted us into a small parlor. After a few moments, Daisy greeted us with a big "Hello Boys, welcome to Daisy Land." I felt like we were in for a very different situation than I was used to.

She greeted us, posed like a starlet in a movie scene. There she stood, a 4½-foot, ninety-three-year-old, frail-looking eighty-pound woman, dressed in a red satin evening gown with gold sequins that normally would be worn at a wedding or other formal event. Later that evening, I figured out what movie she thought she was in.

She asked us to follow her into her dining room, where dinner was about to be served, and asked us to join her. We were delighted at her offer. It had been a very long day's driving, and it was nice to sit down to a home-cooked meal.

Her housekeeper served us a delicious Southern-style meal. The first course, a shrimp and okra gumbo, set the stage for the rest of the meal. The next course, chicken-fried steak with a side of collard greens and biscuits, was divine. For dessert, she served the most incredible sweet potato pie I'd ever tasted.

During dinner, Daisy told us never-ending stories about her life and the long marriage to her late husband. It seemed they had a storybook romance, and she was heartbroken when he passed. They traveled the world together during their sixty-eight years of marriage and collected rare and interesting pieces of furniture and artwork from all around the globe.

After dinner, she invited us into the parlor, where the Steinway was proudly displayed. At that point, we were very tired from our long trip, and our bellies were full of the wonderful meal. I couldn't help noticing all the unique artwork, sculptures, and beautiful hand-carved furniture in the room. She had a wonderful story to go along with every object. The story I found most intriguing was the one she told us about the history of the red velvet curtains that covered the windows in her parlor. She seemed excited to ask me if I was interested in hearing the story behind them. When I told her that I was, she became even more animated.

Sighing deeply, her eyes filled up with tears, but she never let one spill over. She told us about a time when she was thirty-seven years old, in 1939. Her husband took her to see the premiere of *Gone with the Wind* in Atlanta, Georgia, at the Loew's Grand Theater. She said this was one of the best memories she shared with her husband in all the years of their marriage, and she had cherished it for her entire life.

Many years later, she and her husband returned to Atlanta. The seats, curtains, and many other items from the Loew's Grand were being auctioned; everything that had been in the theater when they attended the premiere decades before. She went on to say that the red velvet curtains in the room where we were sitting were made from the stage curtains from the theater. At that moment, I saw her proudly display all of her elegance and grace as the Southern belle that she was.

It was getting late, and up to this point all of the conversation was about her and her wonderfully exciting life. But at this point, it was time to talk about her piano. I was ready to pay her and load the piano onto the truck, grab a cheap motel, get a good night's rest, and start on the long road home early the next day.

I asked her if it would be okay for me to inspect the piano at this time. She replied that she thought it was too late now to do any business, and she would prefer to do it in the morning after we'd all had a good night's rest.

I thought she had a valid point and agreed with her. As we were about to say our good-byes for the night, she asked us if we would care to stay the night in one her guest rooms. I took a moment to discuss this with Michael, and we both agreed it would be best if we stayed at a local motel. Michael had brought along Casey, his beautiful yellow Labrador retriever, and Daisy might not have welcomed the dog in her home.

We thanked her for the dinner and her gracious Southern hospitality and said good night. After a short ride around the town, we found a local motel and settled in for the night.

The next morning, we started the day early with a good breakfast from a local diner and headed over to "Daisy Land."

When we arrived at her home, Michael filled up the dog's water bowl, as he was doing regularly during the trip. He made sure she had plenty of food and water, and walked her before he made her comfortable in the truck. We kept the windows open for her to get plenty of fresh air.

We walked up to Daisy's door and rang the bell. Her housekeeper opened the door as she had the night before and welcomed us in once again. She asked us to follow her into the dining room and said that Daisy would join us shortly. It was now 10 a.m., and I was more than ready to make things happen, as we had a very long drive ahead.

Her housekeeper offered us coffee and some Danish as we sat waiting over half an hour for Daisy to come into the room. This time, she appeared dressed in a white silk evening gown with a bright red scarf. I thought to myself this was getting a little ridiculous but played along, since we were in her house and were being treated like kings.

Again, she started with the stories of her life as the belle of the ball wherever she and her husband appeared for events. Even though she was beaming with new old stories to tell, I had to let her know that I couldn't spend a lot of time there that day, because we had a very long ride back to New York and we wanted to get started soon.

Her smile became a frown at that point. Her words to me were, "You just won't do." I asked her what she meant by that, and she repeated, "You just won't do."

In an effort to stay on track, I asked her if we could please finish with our business, and she asked me what my offer was to buy the piano. I told her that I would be paying her exactly the amount she had asked for when we had spoken. Her answer to that was that she wasn't going to sell it to me for the low price she had given me; that was just a "monkey bid."

"A monkey bid?" I asked her, "What is that?"

"Oh, a monkey bid," she replied, "that's a low offer just to get you in the door."

I replied to her, "So you lied to me?"

She said, "No, I just gave you a monkey bid."

Boiling over, I looked her in the eye and told her that that was a dirty rotten thing to do—making me drive all the way from New York, knowing she was leading me on all that time.

Her reply to me was, "You don't have to buy the piano. It looks fine right where it is." Then she looked at me again and repeated, "You just won't do."

I was so mad I had to take a long walk outside. Michael came with me and we took his Lab for a run. After I blew off some steam running around with the dog, I rang the bell. Much to my surprise, Daisy answered her own front door and invited us in.

This time we were led into the parlor where the piano was. She boldly asked me if I wanted to make her a much higher offer than she'd monkey-bid me. I again told her that it was a very underhanded trick she pulled with her monkey-bidding way of doing business, and that if I had not driven so far on what I took as her good word, I wouldn't even take a look at her piano. One more time she looked into my eyes. She changed her chant to, "You just will NOT do." I was fed up with her and her crooked ways, and only wanted to try to reason with her.

I approached her with kindness and consideration that she didn't deserve. One last time, I asked her how much she wanted me to pay her for a piano whose price we had already agreed on many days before. She replied with a figure that was two times the price she had agreed to. At that moment, I realized there were not going to be any more negotiations. It was now midafternoon, and I was burned out from her trying to make a monkey out of me.

I figured our time there was over and told her I was not interested in dealing with her anymore. Michael and I walked over to the front door, opened it, and walked outside, ready to leave. Daisy asked us if we would consider staying for dinner. Very curtly I answered her that we needed a few minutes to take the dog for a walk but would let her know soon. We both decided we would give it one more try. We thought that by staying for dinner, it would give us one more chance to negotiate the purchase of the piano.

After we took some time with Casey, we went up to her front door and rang the bell. The housekeeper greeted us and invited us in. This time it was all three of us, Michael, his dog, and me.

We were escorted into the dining room. Of course, Daisy was nowhere around, but we knew where she was, putting on, as we imagined, her evening gown for that night. All bets were on her walking into the room like she was playing the part of Scarlett O'Hara, and she had the curtains to prove it! Fifteen minutes into our wait, she gracefully entered the room dressed in a green and gold velvet full-length evening gown, ready to show us who was the boss of "Daisy Land."

Here we were, once again, at her dinner table about to be served, and we hadn't yet made the deal on the piano.

At that moment, I realized we were a captive audience, and all she really wanted was the company that we provided by listening to her life stories and dining with her in the home that held so many great memories for her. The three of us, and even Casey, were in her dining room joking, laughing, and eating good food together. Although she had tricked us, she remained a very charming old woman, caught up and involving us in her memories.

After dinner, she stood up and said, "It's time you bought my piano."

I said to her, "You are correct, but 'you just won't do.'" We all laughed and went into the parlor where the old Steinway D was sitting.

After a few monkey bids of my own, we peacefully and professionally agreed on a price. After a few hugs and a few tears that she managed to hold back, I could see that she was silently reminiscing about the days when her husband and she had enjoyed the lavish lifestyle that made her so happy.

We went to the truck and gathered our moving gear along with the funds that had made her happy.

After the piano was secured in the truck, we said our good-byes. As we were about to walk out the front door for the last time, Michael's very well-behaved yellow Lab decided it was time to leave a gift right inside Daisy's foyer, by dropping a big doggie doo-doo on the floor. We doubled over laughing as we cleaned up the mess and headed toward home.

Chapter 19

NEPPER NEPPERLAND

There is a place where countless numbers of Steinway owners have brought their pianos to be professionally restored by the best master craftsmen. It's a place where Steinway restoration dreams come true.

The Alexander Smith Carpet Mills, a national historic district located in Yonkers, New York, was first built and developed by businessman Alexander Smith over the course of five decades, from 1871 to 1930. It lies along the banks of the Saw Mill River. There are eighty-five buildings in total; nineteen mill buildings and six rows of buildings where the workers were housed. The main mill building was originally built in 1871 and was expanded between 1876 and 1883. It is a three-story rectangular building, fifty-two bays wide and five bays deep in the Second Empire style. The carpet weaving industry was revolutionized by looms invented in this plant by Alexander Smith and carpenter/inventor Halcyon Skinner. Today it is known as the Yoho Art Studios, where more than eighty working artists and crafters display their work.

I was first introduced to this location in 1996, while searching with a team of Steinway piano restoration gurus for a place for them to work and develop a co-op. I envisioned a place where I could employ them to restore the Steinways I was wholesaling to other rebuilders. This way I could offer these outstanding craftsmen a place to work, either full-time or part-time, whichever they preferred. Most of them worked at other facilities that they didn't own or have any vested interest in, never sharing the profit from the work they did. The paycheck they received from their employer was hardly compensation for the painstaking, back-breaking, long hours they endured. I'd met them during the years I supplied the shops where they worked, and I saw and felt their pain. I also worked many years restoring pianos, and I understood what they were going through.

My good friend and partner on this project was Jeffrey Baker. Jeffrey, a very well-known and highly respected piano tuner/technician, was dubbed "The Tuner to the Stars" in New York City. He worked with artists such as Billy Joel, Chick Corea, André Previn, and many others. Our search for such a place brought us to the old carpet factory on Nepperhan Avenue in Yonkers. Together we turned the key, and the New York Piano Cooperative was born.

We started the ball rolling when we rented five thousand square feet of dirt-filled, unpainted factory space on the fourth floor of 540 Nepperhan Avenue. For twelve to twenty hours a day for almost a month, Jeff, my oldest son Michael, and I swept, painted, washed windows, built work tables, hung curtains, and designed a shop and showroom.

Whether happy or not restoring pianos in other shops they worked in, anyone who was experienced in piano restoration was welcome to come here to work. The difference was that we would pay them by the job, not by the hour. We would agree on a price based on their skills and the job they were to do, not an hourly wage. We had many takers, including workers employed at the Steinway factory.

The word on the streets of the New York piano community was out: the guy who supplied the used Steinways to the trade, and the man who tuned for the stars, just set up a shop in Yonkers called "The Piano Cooperative." After a few months of advertising in the *New York Times,* the calls started coming in from piano owners, retailers, technicians, and teachers, all wanting us to restore pianos for them.

I thought it was a good idea to open the shop. It would take me off the road so that I'd be closer to home and spend more time with my family. At the same time, I could once again enjoy working on Steinways. In addition, I would be working alongside some of the best piano restoration experts, and I would sharpen my own skills.

But after two years of putting in many long, hard, exhausting days, often with very little sleep, I concluded that this was not for me. If I went out on the road for a few days to hunt Steinways while Jeff was out tuning for his clients, the work would suffer. The reason was, just as an orchestra needs a conductor, the craftsmen needed someone to coordinate the work. We tried to have enough pianos in restoration to keep the workers busy. Most of them had plenty of work where they were otherwise employed, so I didn't have the burden of having full-time employees to be concerned about. At the same time, if I wasn't turning out enough work to warrant the cost of my overhead, it was a losing proposition.

Once all the Steinways that Jeff and I owned were restored and ready for sale, we opened our factory showroom to the public. We now had eighteen of the most beautiful, regulated, voiced, and finely tuned Steinways ready for retail. The only other place in the New York metro area where you could buy a Steinway of this quality was either Steinway Hall or one of the other piano stores in Manhattan.

We advertised our Steinways in all the local papers, including the *New York Times*. We received many calls from prospective buyers.

The ones that were interested made appointments, but very rarely kept them. We did sell a few through piano teachers in the area, as well as from leads that came from piano technicians who worked for us.

We ultimately realized that the people who bought most of the Steinways, the ones willing to pay the big dollars, wanted to buy from established retailers in New York City. Most of them lived in the city and were a short walk or quick cab ride from those stores. That left us out of the retail end of the business. We were in an industrial area outside of the city, where most people would not come to buy pianos. That was the one thing we hadn't factored in when the plan began. With a showroom full of Steinways that might take longer to sell than I could afford to wait, we decided to liquidate our inventory, but we were able to maintain the restoration segment of the business. With a call to one of the better-known piano retailers in New York, we wholesaled our entire collection.

Once all the pianos we'd restored were gone, the showroom stood empty. We still had a few pianos that were being completed for clients. Our dream of having a full-service restoration shop, including a retail showroom, was over. Well, not really; the shop was still there, as were the people who did the work.

As the word got out that all the finished stock was sold, the workers were concerned about where the next batch of pianos would come from and when they would get there. It wasn't long before they were bringing in their own work from all over the Tri-State area. They all knew that they could go back to work full-time for the shops they worked for previously, or they could stick it out and make the co-op work for them, keeping all the profits for themselves.

Jeff and I packed up our office, our tools, and our burned-out brains. We gave the work tables and the office furniture to the workers who decided to remain. It was time for me to go back on the road to hunt Steinways.

It was a sad moment when I locked the door behind me for the last time. As I walked down the winding spiral staircase to the street below, I looked up at the tall windows that I had looked down from so many times. For a moment I stood and watched the cars driving up and down Nepperhan Avenue, passing the chain-link fence that held the metal sign in the shape of a grand piano lid that read "The Piano Cooperative."

The most amazing thing is that the dream of having a successful restoration shop was not over. At least twelve full-service piano restoration shops have since followed our lead and opened in the old carpet mill on Nepperhan. These shops rebuild and service hundreds of the finest pianos worldwide each year and employ most of the piano technicians and restoration experts in the Greater New York area. Many of them are my friends: Jesus De Los Santos, owner of Emporium Piano Restoration; Luis Cajas and Carlos Macancela, owners of Cantabile Piano Arts Inc.; Joe Hanerfeld, owner of Craftsman Piano Company; Bienvenido De La Cruz, owner of Chulo's Piano Refinishing; and Mikhail Bogomolny, Steinway master action craftsman. I'm proud of the fact that at one point I had the chance to work with all of them.

Ultimately, it worked out quite well for me. I have remained friends with all the shop owners in the complex. They know me and remember that I was the first to turn the key as the leading force in bringing piano restoration there more than twenty years ago. When they need a Steinway for themselves or for one of their prospective clients, they call me.

Nepper Nepperland, a place where my piano dreams really did come true, and still do.

Chapter 20

RACH'S WRAP

In a tiny town located in the Upper Peninsula of Michigan, around the thaw of 1996, I visited with a lovely ninety-year-old woman who told me the best piano story I have ever heard.

I had run an ad in her local newspaper in search of Steinways, and she'd answered my ad. In a British accent, she told me she had an early 1900s model M, a 5'7" mahogany grand that was purchased for her when she was nine years old. She said that she wasn't sure she wanted to sell it, but I was welcome to come and look at it anyway.

I had been traveling through the Midwest, on an eight- to ten-day tour hunting Steinways. I felt it would be worth my while to see her piano.

Several days after she called I finally arrived at her part of the world. The air was fresh and clean, and the landscape was breathtaking with the combination of the tall, mature trees and rugged mountain views. I called her from a local phone booth to let her know I was in the area for the night, and she invited me to come right over.

It was around 7 p.m., and the sun had already set. I found her quaint little house and drove my truck slowly into her driveway. I thought it was best to approach this way, as she was elderly, lived alone, and seemed nervous on the phone.

I rang her doorbell and the door was opened by a short, well-kept, hunched-over white-haired lady. She exuded an air of royalty, and the excitement of a much younger woman.

She invited me into her living room, and she shared some of her family history with me. Then she stood up and led me to her piano.

She asked me, "Do you see the scarf hanging from the brass lamp behind the Steinway?" I looked over at it. It was worn, dark chestnut in color, and tight-knit. I answered, "I see it now."

"When I was ten years old, Sergei Rachmaninoff came to perform at a small theater in the town where I lived. My father had arranged for me to meet him backstage before the concert. When I entered the small room where he was, it was very cold, and he was warming his hands next to a small heater."

She continued, "He stood up, took my hand, and greeted me. He remarked how cold my hands were. Then he took the scarf that he'd been wearing and wrapped it around me. I've kept that scarf hung from the brass lamp next to that piano for eighty years. I was so excited to be able to meet such a famous pianist. I've treasured the memory, along with the gift that he gave me, ever since that day."

After telling me her story, she told me that she could not part with her piano but thanked me for taking the time to listen to her. I asked, "Was the reason you wanted me to come here to see the piano, or listen to your story?"

She smiled and asked, "Well, did you like the story?"

I replied, "I loved the story. I've always admired Rachmaninoff. Would you at least sell me the scarf?"

She chuckled and said, "No. It stays with the piano."

Chapter 21

LOST IN GROUNDHOG TOWN

I received a call from a piano tuner from Punxsutawney, Pennsylvania, with whom I'd never done business. He offered me a Steinway model M 5'7" grand piano and a Steinway upright. We spoke for a week or so about the conditions of his pianos. Finally, we agreed on a price, subject to my inspection.

We planned to meet at his home/shop in the late afternoon of February 1st. Since the weather was unpredictable, I left early that day with my trusted helper, Jeff. I thought I had allowed enough time to drive from my home in Poughkeepsie, New York, to reach his home at a respectable hour. The average driving time was five and a quarter hours, and as I'd figured, snow was falling steadily. When I arrived at his shop, the sun was setting. He made it clear, in a begrudging manner, that he was ready to shut down for the day.

Once we made our introductions, in his very dimly lit attached garage/piano shop, Don pointed out the two pianos he had offered to sell me. I could see the upright in that poorly lit room, but the grand wasn't set up. It was lying on its side, so it was impossible to see its condition. I asked him if we could set it up so that I could see what I was buying.

He became rude and obnoxious, claiming that I was late getting to his shop, and that he didn't want to get involved with setting up the piano. I calmly tried to explain to him that I had been driving a long way in bad weather and had done the best I could. He said that I would have to come back in the morning if I wanted to see what I was buying, or I could trust him that it was what he claimed it to be. I told him that I would have to set it up anyway to put it onto my moving equipment, regardless of its condition. At that point, it would be easy to inspect.

Then he got angry and told me to leave; that he wasn't going to sell me the pianos. I finally lost my temper with him and told him that I had just driven almost seven hours to buy the pianos that he had agreed to sell me, contingent on my inspection.

He became aggressive, raised his hand to me, and told me to get out of his shop and off his property. I raised my hand in defense. Jeff stepped in between us. Jeff was twenty-seven years old, 6'2", and built like a hulk. He told Don to back off or he'd be sorry. It was not a good moment, to say the least. Don finally quieted down once he realized he was being unreasonable. He asked me if I would mind coming back in the morning, and then we would finish the deal. I agreed to his request, and Jeff and I left.

We hadn't planned to stay overnight at a shabby motel in Punxsutawney, Pennsylvania, on February 1st. Getting trapped in the hometown of the famous groundhog known as Punxsutawney Phil on his celebrated day was absurd, as you could imagine.

It never occurred to me that I would be a visitor in the town where Groundhog Day was to take place. The famous groundhog, according to tradition, comes out of his burrow and looks for his shadow. If Phil sees his shadow and returns to his hole, he has predicted six more weeks of winter-like weather. If Phil does not see his shadow, he predicts an early spring.

I was focused on getting the deal done that I had driven so far to make. Jeff and I drove to Don's place to wrap up the deal as quietly and amicably as possible.

When we arrived at his house, I walked up and knocked on the door. Don greeted me with a very different attitude than he had the night before. We set up the Steinway grand, and I inspected it. The piano was in much worse condition than he had described to me over the phone. The veneer on the lid and portions of the case were badly water damaged. Rather than get into another argument with Don, I reluctantly decided to buy it as-is. After we finalized the deal, Jeff and I loaded the two pianos onto the truck. Don and I thanked each other and I drove away, making a mental note not to do business with him again.

As we headed back down the road, I mentioned to Jeff that the landscape didn't look familiar. We'd driven most of the way there on Interstate 80, and that was the highway we needed to get back to.

We drove down the road and through the center of town until we reached a "T" intersection in the road. I pulled over to the side of the road to check the map, but it was nowhere in the cab of the truck. I decided to take a left turn. My sense of direction was very seldom wrong. We drove for about five minutes, and surprisingly came back to the place where I had made the left turn just minutes before. I stopped at the "T" once again, pulled off to the right side of the road, and once again tried to find the map. With no luck finding it, I figured that turning right at the intersection this time would take us to the local highway that would lead us to Interstate 80.

Driving in the opposite direction, we arrived right back at that same "T" in the road. We were completely baffled, and disturbed that we were stuck in Punxsutawney on Groundhog Day.

I don't believe in coincidences, but this had me a little scared, especially considering the date and the town I was in. I wished that I could cut a hole in the universe that would allow me to pass through it, so I could get out of the groundhog's home.

This was going to be my last attempt to get out of Punxsutawney. If it didn't work, I'd have to stop and ask directions—something I rarely ever did. My last attempt was a success. I took the same left-hand turn at the "T" as I had almost forty-five minutes before. This time I also took the next right just after the left. We ended up on the local highway that led us onto Interstate 80, heading east. Some six hours later, I arrived at my front door.

This trip was a life lesson about holding onto my map and never traveling to Punxsutawney on Groundhog Day.

Chapter 22

AMBER WAVES GOOD-BYE TO MISTY

If you drive your car in the state that is the proud home of the "Fighting Irish," you'll see the phrase "Amber Waves of Grain," which is Indiana's motto, on the license plates. Indiana is the crossroads of the Midwest because most of the highways leading in all directions connect in that state. This is where my travels often brought me during the years I was crossing the Great Plains. I went into many homes across the Midwest to buy Steinways and meet with the owners of these precious instruments. I enjoyed listening to them as they shared their stories about the special moments they'd experienced with their Steinways.

During my early years of driving through Indiana, I was fortunate to meet and become close friends with one piano rebuilder who specialized in the restoration of Steinway pianos. Mr. Dennis Chupp lived and worked in the heart of Indiana. In addition to buying and selling Steinways together he, along with his loving family, shared his religious views with me, showing me the other side of a coin that I was not familiar with. To this day, I'm grateful to him for that. To this day I'm very grateful to him for this. What was an even greater connecting factor for us was that I'd met his father, Elmer, almost ten years before. He had been in my home area in New York delivering custom-designed vans to an auto dealership where I was working at the time. Many years into our personal and professional relationship, I felt that our meeting was more than just a coincidence.

One cold and stormy winter afternoon as I was traveling solo on my way back to New York from the Midwest, I pulled into a truck stop just outside of Indianapolis with my half-filled truck of Steinway grand pianos to get some gas. On the way into the truck stop, I saw a woman in a station wagon that was filled with young kids, and a few large handwritten signs taped to the back windows of her car that read "Siamese Kittens for Sale." It was obvious she had little money, driving that old car packed with kids, selling kittens at the local truck stop by the side of the road. I drove in to get my gas and a few other things and headed back toward the interstate. I also had five children back in New York. A few of them were very young, as were her children. I reasoned that if I bought a kitten, I would not only help her with her finances, but it was also a good gift for me to bring home for my children; a kitten they could have fun with, along with giving the cat a good home.

I pulled up next to her car and got out of my truck. She also got out of her car, and greeted me warmly. Looking at the condition of the car and the way her children were dressed, it was easy to see she could use some help. I asked her how much she was asking for the kittens. She replied that they were sixty dollars each, and she only had two left. I then asked how many she had started off with, and she replied the litter was seven to start. In my opinion, if five had already gotten sold at sixty dollars each, she was not doing too badly.

I asked to see the two she had left. Two of her girls, both looking like they were about six or seven years old, held the two kittens out to me from the back of her wagon.

One was a little bigger and more alert than the other. The smaller one was a female, who she told me was the runt, last of the litter born. The other one was a male, who was born somewhere in the middle. The markings of the female were much more distinctive and colorful, and her blue eyes were mesmerizing. She was sweet and calm; the male was much plainer-looking and very anxious. My pick was the little lady. I told the woman I wanted to buy the runt. She was so happy. I paid her the sixty dollars, thanked her, and wished her all the best. Carrying the frightened little kitten back to my cold truck, I held her close to me against my chest. She rested on my right arm until she and the truck both warmed up.

After a few miles of driving, I realized I needed to get her water, food, and a box with dirt in it to make sure she had a place to visit once the food and water went to work. I stopped at the next town off the highway and stocked up on kitten chow, water, small bowls to put them both in, and a few small brown shipping boxes from the store. I filled one up with a little dirt, and she was all set to travel back to New York in kitty comfort.

For most of the almost 900-mile trip home, she sat either tucked between my right arm and stomach, or up on the dashboard, partially blocking my view through the windshield. It was as though she needed to pose for me, so I could see just how beautiful she was.

One thing was certain: she had a very strong need for attention. Except when she was sleeping, if I wasn't showing her complete attention, she would screech a meow that would fill the small passenger cab of the truck until I either took her in my arms or spoke to her soothingly.

Traveling through Ohio and into Pennsylvania, I was exhausted from driving and playing kitty games. It was time to find a room for the night. After checking in, I brought my new friend and all her goodies into what must have been her first night in a motel room. We finally bedded down for the night, me tired from a long day of driving, and she seemingly very secure, tucked in bed with me.

After one more day of driving with the newest member of my large family, I finally arrived in my driveway. I stepped out of the truck with the pretty kitty in my arms and walked into the house. Everyone wanted to hold her first. They all instantly fell in love with her. It was an easy fall!

I'm not sure which one of my children named her. I think it started out as a group effort, and then my youngest daughter, Chelsea, threw it out there. The kitten was instantly crowned "Misty."

For more than four years, she was one of five family pets. There was also Buster, a near and dear companion to me, a mixed-color brown male boxer-shepherd. Millie, our very long-lived black-and-white angel of a cat, was incredibly lovable. Eventually we also had Salem, my oldest daughter Kimberly's young male jet-black cat, who was born to Misty from her first litter (she also had a second). He was a super cool dude who mostly kept to himself, but had no problem showing strong affection. And outside the barn (she refused to go in there), in the paddock area was Lady Bug, Chelsea's horse, a medium brown three-quarters Arabian Palomino. She was a sweetheart that was fun to ride.

During the last few months she was in our home, Misty had difficulty with incontinence, which was also difficult for us. After a few visits to our veterinarian, he explained that this problem was not going to go away, but only get worse. Surgery was not an option, but we could try to find a way to keep her comfortable. Our house now had a foul odor from her heart-wrenching illness. We tried putting cat diapers on her and were partially successful in our attempts to help her stay with us. We hoped to keep her close to us, but it turned into a full-time job for our busy family.

I thought the best thing for her would be for me to take her to the piano workshop where I was working part-time helping a fellow piano man, Frankie Good-Guy, in New York City. There I would make her a comfortable area, with everything she needed for a while. Everyone agreed we needed a break, and that that was the best thing for her.

It was early on a weekday, the kids were getting ready for school, and we all knew this was the day Misty was leaving home. With sad faces they all gave her a hug and said their good-byes. I assured everyone she would have a good home where I was taking her.

I packed Misty up in her carrying case, with a different collection of goods than the ones that had come into our house with her, almost five years before.

It was a real tear-jerker for me when I put her into my car to take her away from the only home she had known. With much loud meowing, she was letting me know about her discomfort. I was doing what I thought was best for her and our family, and hoped it was the right decision for all of us. She rested for the remainder of the short trip to New York City.

The shop where I was taking her was located in the Chelsea district of New York. I found this very poetic, since she was named by Chelsea, and was finding her new home there too. I pulled into the lot that I'd been parking in regularly for over two years. Riccardo, the attendant, who was a real friendly guy, waved me in.

I got out of the car and picked up Misty in her carrying case along with the box filled with her food, water, litter, and toys.

Riccardo came up to me and asked me where I was going with the cat. I gave him a quick version of her story. He begged me to let him have Misty to take home for his elderly grandmother. I explained to him that she was incontinent, and that she had a very hard time controlling her bladder. He told me that his grandmother had the same problem and went on to say that they would make a perfect pair. He then assured me that she would love to have her and would take the best care of her. He pleaded with me, saying over and over that it would save his grandmother's life to have this beautiful cat as a companion.

At that point, I felt that if I didn't give both Misty and Riccardo's grandmother a chance to see if this would work, I would be standing in the way of what was destined to be a blessing for both. I was all choked up as I handed Misty to Riccardo, entrusting him with the dear family cat that I had picked up five years before in that Midwestern Indiana truck stop, when she was just a kitten.

When I got home that evening, I told my family exactly what happened that morning, and that Misty was now in the care of a woman who would love her, take good care of her, and be a companion for her. Even though it hurt us to see her go, we all agreed that it was for the best all around.

I checked in with Riccardo regularly to see how Misty and his grandmother were getting along. He always said they were doing very well, and it was a great thing that we did for both of them.

Chapter 23

BUY A STEINWAY, SAVE A HOUSE

It was during the early hours of the last day before Helen Beaman would be forced to leave her home; the home that had been in her family for over three generations.

I arrived in her driveway, as I'd promised, at two in the morning. With cash in hand, I was there to try to make her worst nightmare turn into the dream she was hoping for.

Two weeks earlier she had called me from an ad that I had placed in her local paper to buy Steinways. She explained that she needed to sell her old Steinway grand piano to raise money to pay her overdue land taxes, or she was going to lose her home by the end of that month. During our conversation, she gave me information about her piano, along with a serial number. I called the customer service department at the Steinway factory, and they verified all the information she had given me. Her piano was an 1878 rosewood Steinway concert grand.

What made this piano so unique was that in that year the first modern-scale, full-plate harp design was introduced. Before that, all Steinway grand pianos had a three-quarter-plate harp design. The maximum tension, for tuning purposes, on the pre-1878 grands was A435 pitch. If the piano was tuned to any higher pitch, the plate might have cracked, and many did. With the full-plate harp design, the piano was able to be brought to A440, and the plate wouldn't crack. A440 is the standard pitch of today.

I only had a few days to check out her piano to see if I wanted to buy it. I also wanted to help her save her family home, and if selling that Steinway piano was the way, I wasn't going to let her down. With little time to spare before her house and piano would be taken to pay her back taxes, I got into my truck along with a trusted helper and headed south.

Her house was a difficult place to find. I had no GPS back then, and I had very limited to nonexistent cell phone service once I reached the farmlands of Clinton, North Carolina. When I finally reached the area, I stopped at a roadside phone booth and called her to get better directions. Although it was very early in the morning, she still wanted me to come over and make her a deal on the rosewood Steinway grand that had been in her home for over 100 years.

Moments later I arrived at the end of her long dirt driveway. As I neared the house, she peered through the curtains of the front door and waved. The old, dilapidated farmhouse looked as if it was about to fall over, but it was the only house she had ever known.

This was the morning of the day her taxes were due. She met me at the door and invited me in. She was very nervous about having a stranger in her house at this hour but knew it might be the only way to save her home.

On her front porch sat a man who looked to be in his fifties, with a cigarette in one hand, a can of beer in the other, and several empty beer cans on the floor around him. To me it was a strange sight at that hour of the morning.

She led me into her living room, where the Steinway proudly stood. I walked over to the old Victorian concert grand. It looked, from the outside, like it was all original, and had never been restored. The varnish had a light crazed patina, which was an indication that it was an original finish. This was the way I liked to buy them. I tried to open the piano to look inside, but it was locked. There was a key sticking out of the lock, which I struggled with to get the piano open. I finally did.

I asked her, "When was the last time this piano was opened?"

She pondered for a moment and answered, "I really can't recall, but it's been about twenty years."

I lifted the large, heavy lid and put the prop stick in place to hold it up. Then I opened the key cover. To my surprise, I found a marvelously well-preserved set of white ivory keys that looked as though they had never been played. I remarked about their fine condition, and she explained, "We always kept the piano closed and locked, so it couldn't be abused by anyone, unless it was going to be played."

Then I looked over the mechanical parts of the piano. It was indeed all original, inside as well as outside. It had been played very little and was in remarkably good condition for its age. In the piano field, we refer to a gem like that as a "Time Traveler."

The house was very run-down inside and out. I felt bad for her. It looked as though she was poor and had little money.

Rather than make her an offer, I asked her, "How much would you need to pay the taxes to keep your home?"

She gave me a number that was almost twice what I would have paid for the piano. Nevertheless, I was there to buy the piano, and at the same time help an old woman keep her home. If that was the only way that was going to happen, I was determined to do it.

With a smile, I agreed to buy her piano for the exact amount she needed to pay her taxes. She was so happy, her eyes filled with tears.

As I walked out to the truck to get the cash, the man on the front porch introduced himself as her son and offered me a beer. That was strange for me because it was around 3 a.m. I accepted the beer nonetheless to celebrate. He got up to go into the house, and I saw that he had a very bad limp in his right leg. Helen took me aside and told me that he was in a very bad motorcycle accident when he was in his early thirties, and never really recovered from it. He was left disabled in many ways.

I paid her the money she needed. Then we packed the piano onto the truck, drank our beers, said our good-byes and I took off down the road to find a cheap motel.

I had bought a Steinway and kept an old woman and her disabled son from ending up in the street. This was one of my most gratifying buys.

Chapter 24

THE WALLPAPERED STEINWAY SECRET

Robert's mother and father had decided to wallpaper their dining room. They went to the store in search of the wallpaper for their finely decorated home. They had lived in Long Island, New York, for over seven years.

Six-year-old Robert thought he could help with this wallpaper project. He started thinking about how he could help without them knowing about it. He figured that if he could get his hands on a few small pieces of wallpaper, he could put them on something in the house where they wouldn't see what he had done, and still feel like he was part of the family project.

When they got back from buying the wallpaper, his mother and father began to mix the paste and measure out the paper. Robert searched for a precious and outstanding prize that he felt would be perfect for his wallpaper project. He chose his mother's 1907 ebony

Steinway parlor grand piano. He was very proud of his choice, since it was one of his mother's favorite things, and he was going to make it beautiful.

The minute he could grab a few strips of wallpaper without his parents catching him, he was going to begin. His mother and father were so busy pasting and hanging, that it was much easier than he'd expected. When the moment came, he grabbed a couple of unused strips of wallpaper without them noticing.

Robert positioned himself under the piano and carefully pasted two strips of wallpaper to the bottom. These two pieces would become the testimony to his part of the project. He went to sleep that night, proud of himself, knowing that he had helped with the family project. The secret lasted many decades on the bottom of the family Steinway.

Almost half a century later, a year or so after Robert's mother had passed away, he was selling me the piano. He told me his secret about the day that he put his mark on the Steinway. He had feared his whole life that his mother would discover it, but she never did.

One last thing he told me was that the place where his parents had bought the wallpaper from was an old-time mom-and-pop hardware store called—drumroll, please—Friedman's! Now, that's synchronicity!

Chapter 25

FROM BEHIND THE CURTAIN

If you've ever visited The Emerald City, it was because you found yourself in a dream after you watched the famous 1939 Hollywood movie *The Wizard of Oz*. I think that everyone who grew up in the United States has seen that movie. The Emerald City is the capital of the fictional Land of Oz in L. Frank Baum's books, first described in *The Wonderful Wizard of Oz*.

One place where you wouldn't want to find yourself in this movie would be the castle of the Wicked Witch of the West. This actually does exist. It's known as Dick's Castle, located in New York State on the Hudson River, across from the U.S. Military Academy at West Point.

One afternoon in the spring of 2010, I received a call from the daughter of one of the most successful men in the travel industry. She asked me if I would be interested in purchasing a non-Steinway piano. After she described the piano to me, and the fact that it was in Connecticut, not far from my home in New York, I decided to go and look at it. I made an appointment to see the piano a few days later.

She had asked me to call fifteen minutes ahead of my arrival, so she could alert the security officer at the main gate. I called, and shortly after I arrived at the security checkpoint, I was instructed to enter through wrought iron gates flanked by large stone pillars. I drove up a long, winding driveway and finally arrived in front of her home. This was one of the most elaborate homes I've ever seen: an immense English Tudor, four stories high, made of stone, with gray slate walkways.

I was met by a caretaker and instructed to drive into a circular driveway and through another gate leading into a courtyard, facing the front door. Once inside the courtyard, I was greeted by the woman who called me about the piano. She invited me into the house. The piano was in a foyer, not far from the front door. After a quick inspection, I decided to buy the piano. We agreed on a price, and I paid her.

During my inspection of the piano, I had been standing next to a brown velvet floor-to-ceiling curtain. Every few moments, from behind it, I would hear the voices of a few women exclaiming "Ooh, ooh, ooh." I asked her, "What is that noise?" She chuckled and replied, "Pay no attention to the voices."

She went on to explain. "Behind those curtains is my father's private museum of Hollywood memorabilia and U.S. Government artifacts. There's a tour group in there right now. If you'll wait a few minutes, I'll take you into the museum and show you around." I was excited that she offered me the opportunity, and waited with her until it was time to go in.

When the tour had moved on, she slowly drew back the curtain and we walked into a dimly lit room. I was standing in front of a very large glass ball that was sitting on an ornate golden pedestal, decorated with flying monkeys. She waved her arm and proudly stated, "I present to you the crystal ball that was used in *The Wizard of Oz*."

Suddenly, the crystal ball lit up, revealing the scenes that I recalled from watching the movie so many times, first as a young boy, and later with my children: Dorothy calling out to Aunt Em for help, and then the Wicked Witch of the West tormenting Dorothy with her threats. It was as though I was there in the Witch's castle. It sent chills through my body, as it had done many times before. I stood there mesmerized, as if I were a child in a movie scene. All I could do was say, "Ooh, ooh, ooh."

Once I got a grip and realized that this was just a fantasy from long ago, she offered to show me some of the other famous pieces of historic value in the museum. I declined, telling her that I was more than satisfied with what I had just seen. She thanked me for buying the piano and I thanked her for showing me the crystal ball from my past.

I slowly drove away from the house, more excited than usual after buying a piano. The child in me still wanted to help Dorothy, the Scarecrow, the Cowardly Lion, and the Tin Man battle the Wicked Witch of the West.

About the Author

Robert Friedman has spent his entire professional career searching for Steinway grand pianos that have been loved and cared for over their many years, and sometimes decades, of ownership. Through his work over the past 40 years, these musical treasures have found their place in the hearts of new owners worldwide. With the help of the thousands of people in his network, his never-ending search continues for Steinways manufactured from 1853 to the present. Robert lives with his wife, Ronnie, in New York's beautiful Hudson Valley. Together they share seven children and thirteen grandchildren, spread far and wide. When he's not on the hunt for pianos, Robert enjoys spending time with his family, traveling, and playing guitars, drums, and pianos.

Bob and Ronnie enjoying life together!

Bob at his father's childhood piano, at 14 months old.